ESSENTIAL VATICAN II

ESSENTIAL VATICAN II

THE COUNCIL FOR THE FUTURE CHURCH

EDITED BY
Christopher M. Bellitto

Paulist Press
New York / Mahwah, NJ

Cover image by AnnaNepaBO / Deposit Photos
Cover and book design by Lynn Else

Library of Congress Cataloging-in-Publication Data
Names: Bellitto, Christopher M., editor.
Title: Essential Vatican II: the council for the future church / edited by Christopher M. Bellitto.
Description: Paperback. | New York/Mahwah, NJ: Paulist Press, [2024] | Includes bibliographical references. | Summary: "This book identifies what has happened in the controversies that have emerged from Vatican II and/or the impact (or not) of the themes/documents in contemporary Church life"—Provided by publisher.
Identifiers: LCCN 2024001816 (print) | LCCN 2024001817 (ebook) | ISBN 9780809156290 (paperback) | ISBN 9780809187928 (ebook)
Subjects: LCSH: Vatican Council (2nd: 1962–1965: Basilica di San Pietro in Vaticano) | Church renewal—Catholic Church. | Catholic Church—Doctrines.
Classification: LCC BX830 1962 .E88 2024 (print) | LCC BX830 1962 (ebook) | DDC 262/.52—dc23/eng/20240715
LC record available at https://lccn.loc.gov/2024001816
LC ebook record available at https://lccn.loc.gov/2024001817

ISBN 978-0-8091-5629-0 (paperback)
ISBN 978-0-8091-8792-8 (e-book)

Published by Paulist Press
997 Macarthur Boulevard
Mahwah, New Jersey 07430
www.paulistpress.com

Printed and bound in the
United States of America

In gratitude for
John W. O'Malley, SJ,
whose life of service and scholarship
offers the model of how to do all
for the greater glory of God

CONTENTS

CONTENTS

PREFACE

This book was inspired by an invitation from Mark-David Janus, CSP, to compile an accessible introduction to Vatican II for the generations born since that most recent general council met 1962–1965. So many of us refer to "The Council" in our classrooms, essays and articles, and public talks, but Fr. Janus wondered if our audiences really know what we mean. We take the event and its aftermath for granted as common knowledge, but that may well be a mistake.

So, we started from scratch. The team of contributors was deliberately drawn from a variety of backgrounds, professional methodologies, personal experiences, and vocations of ministry steeped in the Council. Our hope is that this volume provides a look back and ahead. All the authors followed the same structure: tell the audience the essentials of your topic; explain what happened at Vatican II, with a sense of where those ideas concerning specific themes and documents came from; and most especially, describe what's happened since Vatican II. Viewed from over a half century of experience in diverse cultures, what do we now see as the document's strengths and weaknesses? Where has the document made a difference—or not? Where have its visions been implemented—or not? What have the reactions for and against been—and why? What might the future hold?

The contributors thank the many librarians and archivists who make our work possible at our home institutions and within the interlibrary loan system. We're grateful, too, for the students, readers, and public audiences who listened, sometimes disagreed, and pressed for better explanations, offering their insights to inform us. At Paulist Press, we're grateful to Fr. Janus's invitation, to the skillful editorial shepherding of Mary Dern Walker and Paul McMahon, and to the team that designed, edited, and produced this volume. May all our efforts bear fruit to the vision and promise Vatican II still offers.

Christopher M. Bellitto

INTRODUCTION

Shaun Blanchard

The Second Vatican Council (Vatican II), held from 1962 to 1965 in Rome, is without a doubt the most important twentieth-century event in the life of the Catholic Church. You can even make the case that Vatican II is the most important event in Catholic history since the French Revolution (1789), and maybe even since the Protestant Reformation in the 1500s. Older Catholics, especially those born before 1960, experienced the significance of the Council firsthand, with all the excitement, debate, change, and disappointment it brought. The last sixty years have seen plenty of disagreement about Vatican II's achievements and failures, and what its sixteen official documents mean or don't mean. But no practicing Catholic who lived through it—whether a university student in Santiago, a factory worker in Detroit, a shopkeeper in Paris, a bishop in Nairobi, or a nun in Kolkata—would deny that Vatican II did *something* and did something profound. Vatican II changed the face of the modern, global Catholic Church, and indeed the world at large.

None of these changes were created *solely* by Vatican II in four years in the early 1960s. All of them have a pre-history, sometimes spanning centuries, and a post-history, too, which is what the contributions in this volume will explore. In the wake of the Council, for instance, attitudes toward Protestants and Jews were markedly different. Before Vatican II, the central Catholic act of ritual and worship—the Mass—was predominantly spoken, chanted, sung, and whispered in Latin, with the priest mostly facing away from the people and toward the altar. After Vatican II, Mass became a predominantly vernacular affair in which the people were encouraged to participate vocally. Priests faced the congregation, with the altar between them. Positive attitudes toward the people in the pews reading the Bible, which had been slowly warming, rapidly intensified. Politically, Vatican II jumpstarted the Catholic world in a direction it had generally been heading, that is, toward liberal and social democracy, in a conscious rejection of the totalitarianisms of both right (fascism) and left (communism) that had persecuted the Church and engulfed the world in violence. While understanding the culture and politics of the 1960s is indispensable for understanding Vatican II, we must also recall the Council's close chronological proximity to the cataclysmic Second World War. The Catholic bishops who filed into the opening ceremony in St. Peter's on October 11, 1962, were separated by only seventeen years from the defeat of Adolf Hitler and the dropping of the atomic bombs in 1945.

WHAT IS AN "ECUMENICAL COUNCIL"?

Before we go further, we should define the event. Vatican II was a general meeting of all the Catholic bishops—from Alaska to Korea, Argentina to Poland—with and under the pope, the Bishop of Rome. Such a meeting has only occurred twenty-one times since the time of Jesus and is called a general or "ecumenical" council (the Greek word *oikoumenē* refers to the known or inhabited world). Catholics and many other Christians see the prototype for an ecumenical council in the New Testament. In the Acts of the Apostles, the sequel to Luke's Gospel, an important deliberative meeting is recounted in chapter 15. The Christian community, led by the apostles Peter and James, is considering a series of questions surrounding both doctrine (Christian teaching and belief) and discipline (church practices and the regulative norms for community life). This "Council of Jerusalem" set a standard for what to do when challenges and disagreements arose in the Christian churches: deliberation, debate, and then authoritative ruling by apostolic leaders.

After Emperor Constantine (who reigned from AD 306 to 337) ended the persecution of Christians in the Roman Empire, the bishops, seen as successors to Jesus's twelve apostles, were able to meet openly with imperial protection and support. They convened just outside Constantinople (modern-day Istanbul, Turkey) to address an issue that was seriously destabilizing the Christian churches—that is, the question of Jesus Christ's relationship with God the Father. This first ecumenical council, held in Nicaea in AD 325, authoritatively proclaimed much of what is now known as the "Nicene Creed" and recited every Sunday in countless Catholic, Orthodox, and Protestant churches around the world.

WHY WAS VATICAN II CALLED?

Even though the Catholic Church recognized twenty previous ecumenical councils, when the plump and elderly Pope John XXIII (Angelo Roncalli) announced in 1959 that he intended to convene one, almost everyone was shocked. Most assumed that Cardinal Roncalli had been elected as a stop-gap pope, a breather after the long pontificate of Pius XII (1939–58). Additionally, though Catholics technically believed that ecumenical councils had supreme teaching and legislative authority in the Church, in practice, those powers had been all but subsumed into the papacy. Finally, the Catholic world did not face a clear crisis, like, say, the fracturing of Europe by the Protestant Reformation that brought on the Council of Trent (1545–63).

Pope John XXIII indirectly answered all these questions. He was concerned that the Church was at risk of losing its ability to "evangelize" or spread the gospel of Jesus Christ to the modern world. In this sense, then, a crisis *did* bring on Vatican II—a "crisis of modernity." The young German theologian Fr. Joseph Ratzinger (1927–2022), who in 2005 became Pope Benedict XVI, went as far as to say that key elements of Vatican II formed "an attempt at an official reconciliation with the new era inaugurated in 1789," in reference to the year of the outbreak of the French Revolution. In answer to this broad and generalized "crisis of modernity," John XXIII gave a broad and generalized prescription. In his famous speech to open the Council on October 11, 1962, John called for an *internal* Catholic renewal in the service of an *external* evangelization. His call was grounded in one of his favorite concepts, *aggiornamento*, an Italian word that can be translated as "bringing up to date."

Externally, however, things looked pretty good in many parts of the Catholic world. The United States, for example, was full of thriving parishes and Catholic schools. When one U.S. bishop heard an ecumenical council had been called, he asked "Why break up a winning team?" But there were, in fact, plenty of ominous signs. These were under the surface in some places, and out in the open in others. As early as 1943, two French priests cowrote a book called *La France, pays de mission?* ("Is France missionary territory?"). It was a serious question: whole sectors of French society seemed to view Christianity as an anachronism at best and the Catholic Church as a regressive force. This was somewhat paradoxical since France had produced an explosion of fervent missionary orders (priests and nuns dedicated to teaching and evangelization far from their homes) and was also a center of a theological movement or tendency called *ressourcement*. This style of doing theology and church life sought reform and renewal by going "back to the sources" of the Christian faith—the Church fathers, the liturgy, and most of all, the Bible itself. Pope John was deeply impressed by these *ressourcement* thinkers, many of whom were bright young German, French, and Belgian priests of the Jesuit and Dominican religious orders.

One emphasis of this *ressourcement* movement that John XXIII eagerly supported was ecumenism. In contrast with the generally negative and condemnatory attitudes toward non-Catholic Christians of the past ("triumphalism"), ecumenism called for respectful listening and dialogue rather than monologue, in the hope of formal, corporate Christian reunion. Pope John's explicit endorsement of the path of ecumenism was radical for two reasons. First, it implied that the Church has something to learn from others, things that might cause a reconsideration of Catholic attitudes or even, in some cases, beliefs. Second, papal endorsement of ecumenism was a clear break from past practice, even if Pius XII had allowed for some very limited Catholic participation in ecumenical dialogue in the 1950s. Even before the Council published a single document, John XXIII's endorsement of ecumenism signaled an end to the "counter-reformation" attitude associated with the Council of Trent. Almost from the beginning, then, the fraught issue of *change* reared its head. Can the Catholic Church change long-held attitudes, practices, or even in some cases teachings? This question was at the center of several tense debates at and after Vatican II.

Finally, the fact that this pope was calling for a *Second* Vatican Council at all implied that the First Vatican Council, or at least an exaggerated but prevalent "ultramontane" (papal and Roman-centered) interpretation of it, needed to be balanced.

The pope did not just pay lip service to the idea that he pastored the Church "collegially" alongside his brother bishops—he was concretely modeling collegial governance. John XXIII never challenged the possibility that a pope could teach infallibly. That was settled Church doctrine. But, with classic cheekiness, John pointed out (quite correctly) that the pope was only infallible when he proclaimed solemn doctrine under very specific conditions, "but that is something I will never do," he said.

THE EVENT OF VATICAN II (1962–65)

Sometimes Catholics get into debates over the "spirit" and "letter" of Vatican II. As this book will demonstrate, the Council cannot be reduced to either—it was both a collection of documents and an event that changed the face of modern Catholicism (the Council of Trent did something similar for early modern Catholicism). Regarding the "letter," Vatican II produced sixteen final documents. At the same time, one need only examine what happened during the Council's first session in the fall of 1962 to see the importance of the "spirit" of Vatican II. No documents were promulgated, and yet an agenda was set and a direction charted. This path and direction were the result of not just the written content that was exchanged and debated, but also of the transformative experiences of participants. The voting participants (called "council fathers"), who were mostly bishops, mixed with people from all over the world. Emerging leaders sparred openly with representatives of the intimidating Holy Office, the Vatican department that oversaw Church doctrine. The experience of Catholicism's rich liturgical diversity was displayed in the encounter with non-Roman Catholic forms of worship and liturgical language (e.g., Arabic-speaking Melkite Catholics). Maybe most radically, the council fathers exchanged ideas and mingled with Protestant and other non-Catholic invited observers.

Each of Vatican II's four sessions ran for about three months—from September or early October to late November or early December—something like a college semester. Let us consider each briefly, highlighting some important moments, debates, and personalities. The first session, from October 11 to December 8, 1962, opened with Pope John XXIII's address *Gaudet Mater Ecclesia* ("Mother Church rejoices"), a speech destined for fame. "Good Pope John" reiterated his desire for *aggiornamento* and his ecumenical hopes; he also chastised "prophets of doom" who treated Catholicism like a fortress and saw nothing good outside its walls. These people acted as if they already had all the answers and thus had "nothing to learn" from history, which John called "the great teacher of life."

While no final documents were approved during the first session, it set the agenda of the Council. First, a proposal to reform the liturgy (public worship; the Mass) received landslide approval from the council fathers. The debate over liturgical reform remained measured. In hindsight, this is a surprise: disagreements about liturgy after the Council often got bitter. It was a different theme that caused the first major showdown at Vatican II. The issue was a fundamental one: the way to present Catholic teaching on "divine revelation"—that is, how God reveals Himself to humanity. When a *schema* (draft text) on this topic was presented for debate, most council fathers rejected it. They thought the text reiterated a theology that was dry, impersonal, un-ecumenical, and insufficiently suffused with the dynamic language of the Bible and the Church fathers. These debates, and especially the skirmish over the *schema* on Divine Revelation, underlined and helped bring about the emergence of two basic blocs of council fathers. "Majority" and "minority" have become the established terms to describe these two general camps at Vatican II. These terms are literal, referring to how people voted on documents, and as such are quantifiable (also, to simply call one side "conservative" and one side "progressive" would be too reductive).

A reform-minded majority bloc made up roughly 80 to 85 percent of the council fathers, depending on the issue under discussion. This majority was characterized by broad support for John XXIII's *aggiornamento* ("updating") and the *ressourcement* ("back to the sources") project identified with "new" theologians like Joseph Ratzinger and the French Dominican Yves Congar (1904–95). Important leaders of the majority came from all over the world, but their leaders tended to come from western and northern Europe (Belgian Cardinal Leo Joseph Suenens; German Jesuit Augustin Bea) and from the Americas (Brazilian Archbishop Dom Hélder Câmara; U.S. Jesuit John Courtney Murray).

The minority, on the other hand, generally opposed deviations from the status quo. They were led by men like Cardinal Alfredo Ottaviani (Prefect of the powerful Holy Office), the Sicilian Cardinal Ernesto Ruffini, and the Irish head of the Dominican Order, Michael Browne. The minority was, as the name suggests, small (perhaps 15 to 20 percent depending on the issue), but it was well-organized and bold, drawing much of its strength from Spanish, Portuguese, Italian, and Latin American council fathers. Members of the minority tended to distrust the proponents of *aggiornamento* and *ressourcement*, preferring the established neo-Scholastic way of doing theology that had prevailed in the seminaries since the late nineteenth century. While not closed off in principle from any reform, the minority wanted clear theological statements formulated in close verbal continuity with the recent past, accompanied by condemnations of the "errors" of those outside (and inside) the Church who departed from these formulations.

When the council fathers left for their home dioceses at the end of the first session, these general party lines were recognizable to any observer. When the Council reconvened for a second session on September 29, 1963, Pope John's vision for a council dedicated to *aggiornamento* and ecumenism was still alive, but the man himself was dead. "Good Pope John" had succumbed to stomach cancer in June 1963. The archbishop of Milan, Cardinal Montini, was elected to replace him. Paul VI was a very different character from John, but he made clear in a speech opening the second session that he aimed to walk the trail blazed by his predecessor.

The same fault lines that had appeared over the draft text on Divine Revelation quickly formed when discussion of a document "On the Church" was announced. Debate over that document, named *Lumen Gentium* ("Light of the Nations"), marked the second and third sessions. At issue was the very self-definition of the Catholic Church: What was the role of the laity, who were the vast majority of baptized Catholics? How did the Catholic Church see other Christians, and non-Christians? What is the nature of the episcopacy (the office of bishop), and how does this relate to the pope's authority and ministry?

Session two can boast of the formal promulgation of the first two documents of the Council, the Constitution on the Sacred Liturgy (called *Sacrosanctum Concilium*, after the document's first two words in the official Latin text) and the short decree *Inter Mirifica* (on the Media of Social Communication). The session concluded with a big surprise. Pope Paul VI announced he planned to take a pilgrimage to the Holy Land. After twenty-seven years of the globe-trotting, celebrity John Paul II (pope from 1978 to 2005), it might seem that this kind of thing is a normal part of a pope's job description. But at the time, Paul's decision was innovative. Additionally, Pope Paul was concretely living out an ecclesiology of encounter: as head of the Church, he acted out what it meant to be a "pilgrim church" (to quote *Lumen Gentium*). In this case, Paul led through dialogue with Jews and in ecumenical friendship with Orthodox Christians.

The council fathers certainly had their work cut out for them when the third session opened on September 14, 1964. There was an optimistic energy in the air. The Orthodox patriarch Athenagoras had responded positively to Pope Paul's friendly overtures. Cardinal Suenens's statement that women made up half of humanity ("if I'm not mistaken," he wryly added) led to the inclusion of a small group of women as "auditors" (nonvoting guests) at the Council. The third session can boast of publishing a trio of closely connected ecclesiological texts, that is, documents that considered the nature and mission of the Church. *Unitatis Redintegratio* was a new charter for ecumenism, while *Orientalium Ecclesiarum* considered Eastern churches that were Catholic but not *Roman* Catholic. Both were rooted in *Lumen Gentium*; all three were promulgated on November 21, 1964.

Despite these achievements, the third session was not without tension and drama. Perhaps the most dramatic stretch of the Council, November 16–20, 1964, was nicknamed "Black Week." Pope Paul VI usually observed from the sidelines, but during Black Week he made three big interventions. First, the pope postponed the vote on a controversial document that affirmed religious liberty as a human right. Americans, especially, were seriously perturbed. Second, Paul VI submitted nineteen changes to the Decree on Ecumenism (*Unitatis Redintegratio*). Most were minor, but the optics were bad—a deliberative assembly was unable to deliberate on these unilateral changes to a document that soon after appeared in its name. Finally, Pope Paul ordered an "explanatory note" added to *Lumen Gentium*. This note was not a minor change. It gave a strongly ultramontane reading to the doctrine of collegiality. The minority breathed a sigh of relief—no democratizing Trojan horse would be smuggled in. While the majority was frustrated, they took comfort in the fact that *Lumen Gentium* was not simply a restatement of Vatican I, and their goal of "balancing" that previous council had still, at least partially, been realized.

The fourth and final session of the Council, in the fall of 1965, had the feel of the frantic end to a busy academic semester. Eleven of the Council's sixteen documents were promulgated in these final twelve weeks. As in the previous session, some big ships were brought to port. These concerned not so much the Church's internal constitution and self-understanding, but rather how to apply that self-understanding concretely in dialogue with others and in service to a suffering and divided world. These *ad extra* (external, outward-facing) concerns produced the massive pastoral constitution *Gaudium et Spes*, which featured a grab bag of social, political, and moral topics ranging from sex and marriage to modern warfare to atheism. The reflections, exhortations, and admonitions in the document were undergirded by the ecclesiology that the Council had already sketched in *Lumen Gentium* and by an optimistic theological anthropology (or view of the human person). For *Gaudium et Spes*, God becoming a human being in Jesus Christ compelled Christians to hope for a fundamental widening of the graced possibilities and horizons of humanity.

Certain connected topics got their own documents. A controversial statement on the Jewish people (initially a chapter in the Decree on Ecumenism) was combined with reflections on the other major world religions and published as the declaration *Nostra Aetate*. The text on religious liberty, *Dignitatis Humanae*, navigated the waters of controversy and eventually achieved widespread consensus. That document, a stunning reversal of quite recent church teaching, explicitly claimed to develop church doctrine, a phenomenon recognized and explored in *Dei Verbum*, which was also finally published on December 7, 1965. The next day, Vatican II concluded with a Mass in honor of Mary's Immaculate Conception. One of the most important religious events of the last five hundred years was over. The debate over how to understand that event—and the sixteen texts it produced—was just beginning.

THE RECEPTION OF VATICAN II (1965 TO THE PRESENT)

The reception of the Second Vatican Council—that is, the various ways Vatican II has been understood, implemented, resisted, and debated—is the story of global Catholicism from 1965 to the present. That story is vast, spanning six decades and stretching across the globe: from lecture halls in South Bend, Indiana, to convents in Vietnam, to rural parishes outside Kinshasa. But let's start with the center: Rome and its bishop.

Pope Paul VI always stood behind Vatican II. On balance, he occupied a tenuous, mediating position that often made neither side of a debate fully happy. More liberal Catholics were deeply disappointed with his encyclical *Humanae Vitae* (1968). This reaffirmation of the Church's traditional ban on artificial birth control shocked many Catholics, especially in the northern hemisphere, who believed that the more open and frank debate encouraged by Vatican II, as well as the mere existence of a papal commission to examine the issue of birth control (implying that it wasn't already settled) would lead to official approval of at least some use of contraception. Dissent from *Humanae Vitae* was widespread and in many cases public. It was clear that not only numerous priests, but even some bishops' conferences thought Paul VI's ban was too total and did not adequately account for the rights of conscience and the discernment of married couples. More conservative Catholics cheered Pope Paul's unpopular stand as courageous and even prophetic. But they were sometimes troubled by what Paul VI did *not* do. While he always upheld the letter of official doctrine, Pope Paul did not, in most cases, discipline progressive theologians who challenged traditional church teaching up to and including papal infallibility (as in the case of the popular Swiss scholar, Fr. Hans Küng).

Despite these conflicts, or maybe even because of them, the postconciliar period saw tremendous intellectual vitality and innovation. While non-European voices played important roles at the Council itself, the actual drafting of the texts was usually led by the Germans, Belgians, Italians, and French. After the Council, Catholic theology became truly global. Some of the most important names in postconciliar theology hail from or spent much of their careers in Peru, India, the United States, Canada, Sri Lanka, and Nigeria.

One important symbolic moment in this process of the globalization of Catholic theology was the Latin American and Caribbean Episcopal Council (CELAM) meeting in Medellín, Colombia, in 1968. The document this gathering produced remains a touchstone for liberation theology. Inspired by Vatican II and by living among the Latin American poor, the Peruvian priest Gustavo Gutiérrez published *Teología de la liberación: Perspectivas* in 1971. Something of a founding father of liberation theology, Gutiérrez helped stimulate a conversation that, despite serious controversy and setbacks, has now been positively received at the highest levels of institutional Catholicism.

Women have always played important roles in Catholic theological and intellectual life, but often indirectly, since they were forbidden from the clerical state and rarely admitted to universities. But after Vatican II, and in part because of it, women began to have more intellectual opportunities within the Church's own academic and institutional structures. For example, in 1970, Elisabeth Schüssler Fiorenza was appointed Professor of Theology at the University of Notre Dame, where she cofounded the *Journal of Feminist Studies in Religion*. Today, it is not uncommon for Catholic women to chair theology departments or, increasingly, to sit on pontifical commissions in Rome. English-speaking theology in particular boasts numerous leading female voices.

Nevertheless, the friction between feminist theology and official church positions, especially on issues of gender and sexuality, remains an unresolved tension in postconciliar Catholicism. In 1994, the Vatican document *Ordinatio Sacerdotalis* denied the possibility of women's ordination to the priesthood. This controversial teaching has not ended the fraught discussion over how to incorporate women's voices meaningfully into the governance and ministry of the Church. Today, the Catholic debate centers on the possibility of the ordination of women to the diaconate. Distinct from this debate, but not unrelated to it, are discussions of ordaining married Roman Catholic men to the priesthood, especially in underserved and remote areas of the world like parts of the Amazon.

A key moment in the postconciliar period was the election of the Polish Cardinal Karol Wojtyla as Pope John Paul II in 1978. He was young by papal standards (fifty-eight), charismatic, and extraordinarily energetic. Wojtyla was enthusiastic about Vatican II, where he had been a voting member as a new bishop. As pope, Wojtyla was certainly not timid about asserting narrative control of the reception of Vatican II, especially via the Congregation for the Doctrine of the Faith (CDF), the former Holy Office, which now-Cardinal Ratzinger led for nearly the entire length of John Paul II's papacy. Just a year after his election, John Paul II ended the lengthy Vatican debate with Hans Küng, stripping the Swiss priest of his license to teach Catholic theology. Küng, who had been a star *peritus* (expert adviser) at Vatican II, led a chorus of disgruntled Catholic intellectuals who believed figures like John Paul II and Cardinal Ratzinger, once men of the Council, had betrayed Vatican II and backtracked on the promise of *aggiornamento*. These intellectuals bemoaned the signs that conservatives had regained the initiative and stymied the progressive potential of Vatican II.

To reassert control of the reception of the Council, John Paul II convened an Extraordinary General Assembly of the Synod of Bishops, a body Vatican II had called for. Meeting in Rome in 1985, this group of Catholic bishops and invited experts discussed the legacy, interpretation, and implementation of Vatican II up to that point. Emphasis was placed on the doctrinal authority of the four constitutions, and the assembly cautioned that the "spirit of Vatican II" (a phrase commonly evoked by theological liberals, from the pews to university lecterns) should not be separated from the letter of the sixteen texts. In a lengthy published interview, Cardinal Ratzinger contrasted a hermeneutic, or interpretive lens, of "continuity" with a "hermeneutic of discontinuity and rupture." Given his role as CDF prefect, Ratzinger's emphasis on interpreting Vatican II in continuity with the Church's doctrinal heritage was enforced by papal backing.

While some Catholics felt that John Paul II and the Ratzinger-led CDF were hamstringing ecclesiological renewal, no one could accuse the celebrity pope of failing to find inspiration from the Council in the arenas of ecumenism and interreligious dialogue. In a stunning event that certainly looked more like the spirit of Vatican II than cautious fidelity to the letter, John Paul II hosted a World Day of Prayer for Peace in Assisi in 1986. Thirty-two Christian organizations were represented along with eleven non-Christian religions. Many Catholics were deeply moved by this display of fraternity and goodwill, seeing in the pope's actions a direct fruit of Vatican II reform.

Others were less impressed. Cardinal Ratzinger refused to attend, worried that instead of respectful dialogue, the optics of the event suggested syncretism. Some of those who were suspicious, not just of the Council's spirit but even its letter, were tipped over the edge. In the aftermath of Vatican II, a French archbishop named Marcel Lefebvre rallied traditionalist opposition around himself. Formerly an active figure in the Council minority, Lefebvre responded to the Assisi conference with his typical rhetoric. "They have uncrowned him!" cried the reactionary Frenchman, in reference to "Christ the King." Nearing the end of his life, Lefebvre was desperate for his resistance group, the Society of St. Pius X (SSPX), to continue. He thus took the risky step of consecrating four of his priests as bishops without Rome's permission. John Paul II responded with excommunication. While these excommunications were eventually lifted in 2009, the organization remains in a *de facto* schismatic situation. Ratzinger, for all his conservatism, never wavered on the demand that traditionalists accept Vatican II without qualification, including the Council's development of doctrine on religious liberty.

These examples show that the reception of Vatican II was—and remains—complicated. Unfortunately, postconciliar reception is too often caricatured through unhelpful binaries of black and white, good guys and bad guys that obscure the pluriform realities of a global Church. However, for descriptive purposes, we can summarize the formation of at least four basic paradigms of conciliar interpretation that took shape within the first two decades after Vatican II's close and endure to this day.

The first is a Traditionalist Paradigm that is either suspicious of the Vatican II texts or openly rejects them. SSPX is the most obvious example. They are a distinct group (and a relatively small one), but softer forms of this paradigm are much more widespread in postconciliar Catholicism, especially in the United States, France, and pockets of Latin America. Often characterized by attachment to preconciliar liturgical forms (i.e., the Latin Mass), Traditionalist Paradigm Catholics seek to mitigate the perceived damage wrought by the Council and its (allegedly) trainwreck implementation. Vatican II, for them, did too much and changed too much.

A second interpretation we can term the Failure Paradigm. These progressive Catholics are unhappy either with the Council's texts or with a perceived betrayal of the positive reformist spirit of Vatican II. Some Failure Paradigm Catholics point to compromises during the Council itself, where the minority managed to take the wind out of the sails of reform before Vatican II had even concluded. Postconciliar events garner significant blame, too: from disappointment with *Humanae Vitae* to the censoring of liberation theologians and other prolific progressives, to the general tenor of the papacies of John Paul II and Benedict XVI. Failure Paradigm Catholics have a well-rehearsed litany of grievances explaining how and why John XXIII's promising, Spirit-led quest for *aggiornamento* was halted and reversed. In an exact inversion of the traditionalist position, the Failure Paradigm would hold that Vatican II, perhaps in its texts but definitely in its implementation, did and changed too little.

Most mainstream Catholic interpreters of the Council, especially those who hold official positions within the Church, would fall into either a third or a fourth paradigm. We can term the third paradigm Spirit-Event. These Catholics accept or celebrate the Council, but with a prioritization of the spirit of Vatican II, an insistence on doctrinal change and innovation, and an understanding of the Council as primarily an event. I call the fourth and final paradigm Text-Continuity. This paradigm accepts or celebrates Vatican II, but with a prioritization of the final texts, an emphasis on doctrinal continuity, and an understanding of the Council as primarily the promulgation of a body of teaching. These two mainstream paradigms do not disagree over accepting Vatican II, or even over whether the Council was a good thing. Friction often hides underneath the surface in discussions of *why* the Council was a good thing, whether Vatican II has been properly implemented, and what this legacy means for the future. For Spirit-Event interpreters, on the one hand, not just the texts but also the new attitudes and orientations associated with the Council helped the Church positively transition out of a defensive mentality to dialogue with and evangelize the modern world. On the other hand, for Text-Continuity interpreters, the actual meaning of the documents must be, in a sense, recovered—that meaning has been obscured by much of what is associated with the spirit of Vatican II. The Spirit-Event approach always seeks to lean forward a bit; the Text-Continuity perspective is a bit more grounded in the past.

These two mainstream paradigms coexisted throughout the long pontificate of John Paul II, sometimes engaging in fruitful and constructive debate, and other times degenerating into polemics. Conciliar projects like ecumenism, interreligious dialogue, and evangelization were always, however, taken seriously. For example, despite his reputation as a centralizer and even an autocrat, John Paul II promulgated *Ut Unum Sint* (1995), a heartfelt cry for ecumenical discussion surrounding the office of the papacy. In 1999, the Joint Declaration on the Doctrine of Justification—a doctrine of central importance in Martin Luther's break with Catholicism—was signed by representatives of the Lutheran World Federation and the Catholic Church. Cardinal Ratzinger, the supposed champion of strict continuity, was instrumental in getting this remarkable ecumenical agreement over the finish line when it stalled.

Competing receptions of Vatican II came to the surface with a vengeance around the new millennium. In 2001, Ratzinger's CDF published a "Notification" critical of the "Christian pluralism" of Jacques Dupuis, a Belgian Jesuit who had taught in India for thirty-six years. The declaration *Dominus Iesus*, a CDF document published the previous year, similarly criticized several "relativistic" tendencies in Catholic theology regarding interreligious dialogue, Christology, and ecclesiology. To Spirit-Event interpreters, *Dominus Iesus* was small-minded, needlessly insensitive to non-Catholics and non-Christians, and backtracked on the spirit of John Paul II's Assisi conference. Text-Continuity Catholics praised *Dominus Iesus* as a careful statement of the Church's most basic convictions, in line with Vatican II, rightly interpreted (as they saw it). Cardinal Ratzinger's public spat in the pages of the British Catholic periodical *The Tablet* with Cardinal Franz König perfectly illustrated this impasse—both men were veterans of the conciliar majority, and each seemed irked and genuinely perplexed by the position the other took regarding the Dupuis Affair.

Ironically, it was Joseph Ratzinger, soon after his election as Pope Benedict XVI in 2005, who gave papal sanction to a kind of ceasefire between the Text-Continuity and Spirit-Event paradigms. In his Christmas address that year, Benedict offered a nuanced evaluation of the legacy of Vatican II, contrasting an unhealthy hermeneutic of "rupture" (whether progressive or traditionalist) with a healthy hermeneutic of "reform." Reform, however, was not just equivalent to continuity. Benedict recognized that at Vatican II "a kind of discontinuity emerged," and indeed needed to emerge, in light of modernity. A "hermeneutic of reform," for the new pope, included both continuity *and* discontinuity, albeit "on different levels."

In a move that shocked the world, Ratzinger retired from the papacy on February 28, 2013. He was the first man to do so since 1415. This act of humility also closed a chapter in the history of the Catholic Church. The man who succeeded Benedict epitomized a new era. Pope Francis (Jorge Bergoglio) became the first Bishop of Rome born outside Europe for over a thousand years. Francis is also the first post-Vatican II pope, in that he is the first pope after the Council to have not attended or participated in the event in any way. Indeed, Bergoglio was not yet ordained a priest when Vatican II closed in 1965. For Francis, the Catholic Church in which he ministers *is* the Church of Vatican II, and he has little interest in arguing about it. He asserts conciliar ideals and orientations as givens and moves forward.

Three phenomena mark the reception of Vatican II for global Catholicism in the pontificate of Francis. The first is a resurgence of opposition to the Council in some Western countries, an opposition waged through the proxy war over liturgy. In 2007, Pope Benedict granted unprecedented latitude for the celebration of the preconciliar Tridentine Latin Mass, as a nod to the richness of the Church's tradition and to bring traditionalist Catholics into more normalized relationships with parish communities, thus undercutting the temptation of schism and extremism. Francis essentially reversed this permission in *Traditionis Custodes* (2021), which caused great controversy and debate over the Council and its legacy in certain quarters.

But, for most Catholics, such debates are a tempest in a teapot. Far more significant is a second phenomenon: the Church's response (or lack of response) to the horrifying revelations of clerical sexual abuse that have rocked much of the Catholic world for over two decades. Beginning with the *Boston Globe*'s 2002 investigation into a cover-up culture in the Archdiocese of Boston, successive waves of crisis surrounding clerical sexual abuse have engulfed the Catholic Church around the world. The credibility and relevance of Vatican II, a council that promoted the leadership of diocesan bishops, empowered the laity, and sought to renew the Church in holiness, hangs in the balance. The Council should be credited with real ecclesiological advances. Nevertheless, without a culture of transparency and accountability at all levels, such advances feel like rearranging the deck chairs of the Titanic in the face of the horror of the abuse crisis.

Finally, the legacy of Francis's pontificate is tied up in his attempt to institute synodality as a normative ecclesiological culture. In evoking synodality, Pope Francis's goal is to jump-start the Catholic Church on a path of ecclesial listening, dialogue, and Spirit-led discernment at every level, from the local parish to dioceses to Rome. For Francis and his supporters, the ecclesiological renewal of Vatican II is an unfinished project, and the path of synodality that this pope calls for is his attempt to receive the Council for a global Catholic Church in the third millennium. How such a project is achievable within a deeply ingrained culture of Roman centralism, or with the recent phenomenon of popes enjoying celebrity status, is not obvious. Nevertheless, if the history of the Catholic Church teaches us anything, it's that this remarkable institution somehow, against heavy odds, manages to change just enough to stay the same.

1

LITURGY

Rita Ferrone

Sacrosanctum Concilium, the Constitution on the Sacred Liturgy, was the first document that the Second Vatican Council produced, and arguably the most far-reaching. It stated the goals of the entire Council and expounded the place of liturgy in the economy of salvation before going on to mandate a thoroughgoing reform of the Eucharist, the sacraments, the Liturgy of the Hours, and the liturgical year. It set the norms, both theological and practical, that would guide these reforms. It also provided guidelines and principles for the renewal of music, art, and church architecture, and prescribed a serious pastoral-liturgical formation for priests, religious, and the lay faithful.

The document has had a lasting significance. It was not only the end of a long process of study, prayer, reflection, and experimentation—the work of the Liturgical Movement over the first half of the twentieth century—it was also the beginning of a monumental project focused on implementing these directives faithfully, both in spirit and in letter. *Sacrosanctum*

Concilium inaugurated a rewriting of the liturgical books that would continue, with tangible results. It also created a mindset concerning what liturgy is, and a hierarchy of values concerning how it should be celebrated.

The reform of the liturgy took shape and was enacted after the Council adjourned, incorporating insights from all the other Council documents as well as from *Sacrosanctum Concilium*. For example, ecumenical sensitivity and respect for the Jewish people influenced key decisions; one sees a renewed emphasis upon Sacred Scripture in the rites; a baptismal ecclesiology emerges through how the assembly and various ministries are treated; themes of Catholic social teaching appear in the prayers, and more. Because of this, the liturgical reform also has a credible claim to being the sign and symbol of the entire work of the Council. In his apostolic letter written on the twenty-fifth anniversary of the Council, Pope John Paul II, echoing the 1985 Synod of Bishops, observed that "for many people the message of the Second Vatican Council has been experienced principally through the liturgical reform." Even today, *Sacrosanctum Concilium* continues to shape our understanding and practice of liturgy. The principles it articulated also give the Church a charter for future renewal—not only renewal of the liturgy, but also renewal of the faith of the Christian people.

THE "SUMMIT AND SOURCE" OF THE LIFE OF THE CHURCH

What was at stake in the liturgical reform of Vatican II? It wasn't just about "moving the furniture" or making a few minor improvements in how we celebrate. The Council sought to get down to the roots of liturgy and reinvigorate the whole enterprise from the bottom up, making clear those foundational principles that had been clouded over, or lost, through time.

One of the foundational principles that the Council wanted to make clear is simply that liturgy is central to the Christian life. Everything else in the life of the Church revolves around it. Prior to that time, although the Sunday obligation was observed, the spiritual life of the faithful often centered more on devotions than on the liturgy itself. The constitution expressed the centrality of the liturgy by saying it is "the summit toward which all the activity of the Church is directed, and the source from which all her power flows."

The liturgy, of course, is not everything that the Church does: there is a necessary place for private prayer and devotion, good works, and communal acts of charity and justice. The point is that *all* the efforts of the Church to spread the gospel and live the Christian way of life ultimately lead us to the liturgy. This is where we offer to the Father everything that we are and all that we do, united to the perfect self-offering of Christ on the cross. Because the liturgy embodies the priestly action of Jesus Christ himself, working through his body, the Church, nothing else equals it in kind or degree. This is why it can be described as the *summit*.

The liturgy is also the *source* of the Church's life. From baptism onward, grace flows through the liturgy to strengthen us as a people, creating a community of faith. "An abundance of graces" comes to us through the liturgy, according to the constitution. Using a beautiful image, the document says that grace is "poured out on us, as from a fountain."

When the Constitution on the Sacred Liturgy speaks of the liturgy as the priestly act of Christ, it embraces both the role of the ordained minister who presides over the liturgy, and the role of the priestly people who join with him in prayer and worship, offering themselves along with the sacrifice on the altar. The constitution enumerates four ways in which Christ is present in the liturgy: through the priest who ministers, the word of God proclaimed and preached, the assembly as they pray and sing, and in an outstanding way Christ is present under the forms of consecrated bread and wine in the Eucharist.

Three of these "presences" were enumerated in Pope Pius XII's encyclical on the liturgy, *Mediator Dei*, in 1947. The one that is new in *Sacrosanctum Concilium* is the affirmation that Christ is present in his word. The Council recommended a "warm and living love of Scripture" and mandated that "richer fare" should be offered to the people at "the table of God's word." After the Council, lectionaries were greatly expanded, and readings were assigned for daily Mass and all the sacraments. By lifting up the Scriptures, the constitution reminded us that in the liturgy "Christ is still proclaiming his gospel" and moved the Church in an ecumenical direction.

The liturgy is a sign and instrument of the Church's unity, as the Decree on Ecumenism would later affirm. The liturgy also empowers the Church to be an efficacious sign of the presence of God in the world—what the Dogmatic Constitution on the Church (*Lumen Gentium*) would later call "the Church as sacrament." The effects of the liturgy therefore go well beyond the celebration itself. They strengthen the faithful to "preach Christ," that is, to evangelize, sharing the good news of salvation. Thus, the restoration of the liturgy to its original vigor, promised by *Sacrosanctum Concilium*, was aimed at achieving all four goals articulated by Pope John XXIII when he called for the Council: Church renewal, updating to the times, ecumenism, and evangelization.

"FULL, CONSCIOUS, ACTIVE PARTICIPATION"

When the council fathers discussed how liturgy ought to be celebrated, their priority was the "full, conscious, active participation" of the faithful. They did not want the people to be present at the liturgy as "strangers or silent spectators." Liturgy, rightly understood, is a communal act. In other words, it is not a sacred performance conducted on our behalf by the priests or other ministers while we maintain a reverent silence as we observe them. Rather, the liturgy is a corporate action in which everyone has a part.

The agreed-upon goal at the Council was that the people, with the help of their pastors, should take part in all the words, gestures, and actions of the liturgy that are proper to them, engaged with the meaning of the sacred rites, and "enriched by their effects." The document is precise in saying of the participants that "their minds should be attuned to their voices," so that inward and outward engagement with the liturgy will be well-integrated.

Pope Pius X had endorsed active and conscious participation as early as 1903. This inspired many in the early Liturgical Movement. But the principle of participation runs deeper than a statement by a particular pope. It is part of the nature of liturgy itself. Liturgies, as *Sacrosanctum Concilium* explains, "are not private functions." Even in the case of small celebrations, we should be aware that liturgy is essentially an ecclesial act.

The Church at Vatican II was also increasingly aware of being a global Church including people of widely different cultures. *Sacrosanctum Concilium* therefore provided for adaptation of the liturgy to the various peoples of the world, a task now known as inculturation. This would further enable full and heartfelt participation. Permission for more use of "the mother tongue" in the liturgy would also enhance participation.

The call to participate appears often in the constitution. As Cardinal Joseph Ratzinger (later to become Pope Benedict XVI) rightly asked in his 2000 book, *The Spirit of the Liturgy*, the important question is: "What are we participating in?" The constitution gives the answer to this question in no uncertain terms. We are participating in the paschal mystery of Jesus Christ. The paschal mystery—his passion, death, resurrection, and glorification—stands at the center of all that we celebrate in the liturgy. We touch the saving mystery of his dying and rising here. The paschal mystery is key to understanding the theology of the constitution. As theologian Angelus A. Häussling observed, it is the "heart-word" of Vatican II.

WEAKNESSES OF THE DOCUMENT

Sacrosanctum Concilium passed overwhelmingly with 2,147 votes for and only 4 against. Pope Paul VI was adamant about achieving something close to unanimity for the documents, so that the impact of the Council would be unifying. The final drafts upon which the fathers voted were therefore sometimes crafted using a strategy of balance concerning provisions that were controversial. While this might seem to be a success—the Constitution on the Sacred Liturgy *did* pass overwhelmingly—it also means that the document "straddled the fence" on certain issues. This would eventually prove to be a weakness. Professor George Lindbeck, an ecumenical theologian and an official Lutheran observer to the Council, pointed this out early on. He was concerned about the long-term health of the reforms ushered in by the Council (in all areas, not only the liturgy), because those who *favored* progress on a given issue and those who *opposed* it could both appeal to the documents in support of their position.

The place of Latin in the liturgy, for example, was a hotly contested question at the Council and the subject of some debate. Archbishop Annibale Bugnini, who worked behind the scenes from 1948 to 1975, organizing the reform and forwarding the liturgical commitments of three popes (Pius XII, John XXIII, and Paul VI), explained that both values (for and against the vernacular) were included in the final text. "We wanted both views to be in there," he said, "so that history could decide." After the Council, a small amount of vernacular was permitted in the liturgy. It was received with great success. Then the floodgates opened. Requests poured into Rome from bishops all over the world for permission to celebrate the liturgy entirely in the language of the people. These were granted, and again this development met with success among the people and even some relief among the priests! A fully vernacular liturgy was ultimately and officially affirmed by papal authority as a genuine expression of the renewal and participation that Vatican II desired. By all accounts, history decided.

Yet, at the same time, the text of the conciliar document says that Latin would remain the language of the liturgy. This allowed a narrative to develop claiming that those who implemented the liturgical reform actually betrayed the Council. Similar tensions arose in other contested areas, such as communion under both forms, the translation of liturgical texts, and the practice of liturgical inculturation. "Sound tradition and legitimate progress," the two values held up by *Sacrosanctum Concilium* as necessary characteristics of the reform, have been held in a delicate and often difficult balance since the Council. The document itself cannot resolve these tensions. Leadership beyond the Council document continues to be needed.

RECENT DEVELOPMENTS

A great deal has happened in the years since *Sacrosanctum Concilium* was promulgated in 1963. We will not review all the developments of these years, but it is worth noting that there have been five instructions on "the right implementation of *Sacrosanctum Concilium*" since the Council. The first three came out within a few years of the Council itself (1964, 1967, 1970). They contained some important practical directives, such as the instruction that new altars are to be freestanding so that the priest can walk around the altar and celebrate facing the people, and that women could serve as lectors. They were brief and not very controversial.

The last two instructions, which came out in 1994 (*Varietates Legitimae*, on inculturation of the liturgy) and in 2001 (*Liturgiam Authenticam*, on the translation of liturgical texts) were much longer and quite different in tone and style from the earlier instructions. The most significant difference was their push to centralize control in Rome. The idea expressed in the constitution was that inculturation would go on locally, and so would the process of translation into the living languages, with only light oversight from the central authorities. In reaction against the Council, however, such decentralization was becoming suspect and even a cause for alarm among the more conservative cardinals in Rome during the waning days of the pontificate of John Paul II. *Varietates Legitimae* set up a number of hurdles to inculturation of the liturgy by insisting on centralized oversight. Many petitions for inculturation were sent to Rome over the years, but they received a chilly reception and almost none were permitted. It was therefore striking when Pope Francis approved the development of a rite for the peoples of the Amazon in 2020, returning to the more decentralized vision of the constitution.

The 2001 instruction on translation, *Liturgiam Authenticam*, also provides a good example of a shift to centralized control. It called for an exact, word-for-word translation of liturgical texts, rather than a concept-for-concept translation as had been pursued in the past (known as dynamic equivalence). In a bold contradiction to *Sacrosanctum Concilium*, the process of approving translations was altered. Rather than allowing authority to rest with the local bishops' conferences, as it had for forty years, the Curia claimed control. The instruction went so far as to say that if the Roman authorities were not satisfied with a translation approved by local bishops, they would issue their own translation and the bishops would be obliged to use it.

In a blow to ecumenism, the document also advised that translations that were similar across denominational lines would confuse the faithful and should be avoided. Catholic participation in ecumenical projects had aimed at achieving common texts. This had been a highly successful tool in developing Christian unity. Because of *Liturgiam Authenticam*, Catholic involvement in such ecumenical projects was immediately withdrawn.

The instruction launched a massive project: retranslating all of the texts of the liturgy from scratch. The highly literal translations produced according to the new norms, however, were often awkward and sounded artificial. When local bishops' representatives petitioned to retain older translations of certain prayers that they deemed more suitable, their requests were denied.

When Pope Francis was elected in 2013, he inherited a situation that was still considerably tense regarding translation. The instruction, not surprisingly, was vastly unpopular. In some instances, dialogue had broken down, as several bishops' conferences were unwilling to implement translations that they felt were foisted upon them, arguing that they did not represent the best of their language and culture. The Congregation for Divine Worship was unwilling to budge. In 2015, Francis assembled a committee to study the question. After receiving their recommendations, he issued the *motu proprio, Magnum Principium* (2017). This returned decision-making authority to the bishops' conferences, as *Sacrosanctum Concilium* had directed. He also urged a more "trustful cooperation" between the bishops and the dicastery charged with the liturgy. While affirming the need for accurate translations that convey the fullness of meaning found in the Latin text (which was the main contention of *Liturgiam Authenticam*), Francis also said that vernacular languages must be respected. The most important principle (the *magnum principium*) is comprehension, that is, the transmission of meaning. Translation must serve active participation. The principles of *Sacrosanctum Concilium* guided the decision and resolved much of the tension.

Sacrosanctum Concilium taught that lay people exercise liturgical ministries in their own right, and not as a delegation of the role of the priest. Since lay liturgical ministries flow from the sacrament of baptism, rather than holy orders, in principle these ought to be open to both men and women. But the inclusion of women was slow in coming.

A good example of this delay is found in the reform of the "minor orders." These ancient liturgical roles were not intrinsically connected to the sacrament of holy orders, although they had for some time been solely conferred on candidates for holy orders as part of the "*cursus honorum*" leading to priesthood. In 1972, Paul VI changed the name from "minor orders" to "instituted ministries." He defined the instituted ministry of lector and acolyte as lay ministries and encouraged their use. Unfortunately, for reasons that are unclear, he limited these two instituted ministries to men. Women were already serving as lectors, and John Paul II later admitted women to serve as acolytes as well, but because of Paul VI's decision they were never permitted to serve as *instituted* ministers.

The Synod on the Word of God (2008) and the Synod on the Amazon (2019) both asked for women in these ministries to be admitted to the instituted ministries in recognition of their gifts and service to the liturgy. But it was not until 2021 that Pope Francis judged it "opportune" to change Canon 230 §1, dissolving Paul VI's restriction. His *motu proprio Spiritus Domini* refers to "the royal priesthood of baptism" shared alike by women and men.

On the Use of the Pre–Vatican II Liturgy

A true liturgical reform replaces the liturgy that predated it. It does not merely construct an optional alternative. The liturgical reform that flowed from *Sacrosanctum Concilium* was undertaken as such a reform. Paul VI allowed priests who were elderly or infirm to continue to celebrate the older rites as they had all their lives, but he was adamantly opposed to offering the same permission to traditionalists, who refused to accept the reformed liturgy in principle. He maintained that to reject the liturgical reform that the Council had mandated was to reject the Council itself "through a symbol," and he would never permit it.

With the passage of time, however, John Paul II began to consider offering permission for small groups to celebrate the pre–Vatican II liturgy in order to reconcile the traditionalists to the authority of Rome. He wanted to lure them away from the Society of Pius X, founded by Archbishop Marcel Lefebvre. The pope took a survey of the world's bishops, but the results were not encouraging: just 1.5 percent of the bishops favored this course. The rest disagreed: they believed it would be divisive. John Paul went ahead anyway, with the support of the

Congregation for the Doctrine of the Faith, led by Cardinal Ratzinger. Despite this accommodation, Rome's relationship with the SSPX reached a breaking point in 1988, when Lefebvre illicitly ordained four bishops. John Paul excommunicated him and the bishops he ordained, but he wanted to extend an olive branch to any members of the Society who desired to remain in union with Rome. So, he expanded access to the older rites and erected the Pontifical Commission *Ecclesia Dei* to oversee such communities.

When Cardinal Ratzinger became Pope Benedict XVI, he took a quantum leap forward in legitimating a wider use of the older rites. In his 2007 *motu proprio*, *Summorum Pontificum*, he gave permission for any priest to use them in private and urged pastors to accede to the request of any group of people desiring the liturgy according to the older books. Not only was the "old Latin Mass" permitted, but the sacraments and the Liturgy of the Hours from before Vatican II were permitted as well. He coined a new term for the older rites: the "Extraordinary Form of the Roman Rite," and called the reformed liturgy the "Ordinary Form." He expected the two forms to coexist peacefully and be mutually enriching. In the ensuing years of Benedict's papacy, bishop candidates who were sympathetic toward the older rites were given preference, and every effort was made to support an unfettered reintroduction of the prereformed rites into practice (over the misgivings of several bishops).

Benedict presented *Summorum Pontificum* as a pastoral and reconciling gesture. What he did not foresee, but which unfortunately happened, was that the fears of the bishops who opposed the permission were realized. Having two forms of the Roman Rite at the same time was indeed divisive. Not only were there two different missals, lectionaries, liturgical calendars, and arrangements of the sanctuary at play; there were also two different mentalities and attitudes toward the reforms of Vatican II. There were even two different catechisms: one informed by Vatican II, and one not. Small wonder, therefore, that the permissions created a "church within the Church."

Rather than becoming more accepting of the Council, many who availed themselves of Benedict's generous pastoral accommodation hardened in their opposition. Some argued that the newer rites were irreverent and heretical and needed to be junked. Others took a more irenic view and worshipped in both communities. But the idea that the Church could have a true reform in one setting and totally put it aside in another was at root destabilizing and, ironically, untraditional.

Pope Francis surveyed the world's bishops concerning how the "two forms of the Roman Rite" were going, and the results were disturbing. He felt that he had to step in for the sake of the unity of the Church. In 2021, he issued the *motu proprio*, *Traditionis Custodes*, abrogating *Summorum Pontificum*. Francis has continued to permit some use of the older rites on a limited basis, but not in the parishes. The readings must be proclaimed in the vernacular, from modern biblical translations. Permission for priests to use the older rites must be approved on a case-by-case basis by the Dicastery for Divine Worship.

The withdrawal of Benedict's broad permissions caused consternation among those who were encouraged to believe that they could worship indefinitely according to the older rites. The process of receiving *Traditionis Custodes* has therefore been challenging. Pope Francis charged the bishops as "guardians of the tradition" (which is the meaning of *traditionis custodes*) to safeguard the living tradition expressed in the reformed liturgy and—as difficult as this may be—to lead their people to embrace the current liturgy across the board. On the positive side, this has been a dramatic reinstatement of Vatican II as the measure of our common liturgical life.

Francis followed this *motu proprio* with an apostolic letter on liturgical formation in 2022, *Desiderio Desideravi*. His rich reflection makes frequent reference to *Sacrosanctum Concilium* and treats it very much as a living legacy. These two statements together are part of a single effort by Pope Francis to strengthen the foundations of a unified liturgical practice, grounded in Vatican II.

CONCLUSION

In looking over the developments of the past quarter of a century there has clearly been a reaction against the Council and its liturgical reform, but it is equally clear that the Council's document on the liturgy has stood up well under the pressure of reaction. No document can do everything. Much depends on church leadership and discernment in changing circumstances. But what a document can do the Constitution on the Sacred Liturgy has done: it provides a touchstone for faithful and creative responses in changing circumstances.

How will the constitution remain a vital part of the Church, once those who remember the Council firsthand pass from this life? One might look to the example of Pope Francis to see how this could work. Pope Francis has demonstrated that he is truly a Vatican II pope, even though he is the first pope since the Council who did not attend the Council. He understands its teachings and uses them as trustworthy guidance and inspiration for the future. The teachings of the Council are not frozen in time. Rather, by discerning the call of the Spirit, the Church today is well capable of bringing them into the future. The fact that Francis's pontificate has been supported by the great majority of Catholics and widely admired even outside the Church is an affirmation not only of himself as a person, but of how he represents the ideas and ideals of the conciliar Church.

FOR FURTHER READING

Faggioli, Massimo. *True Reform: Liturgy and Ecclesiology in Sacrosanctum Concilium.* Collegeville, MN: Liturgical Press, 2012.

Ferrone, Rita. *Liturgy: Sacrosanctum Concilium.* Mahwah, NJ: Paulist Press, 2007.

Grillo, Andrea. *Beyond Pius V: Conflicting Interpretations of the Liturgical Reform*. Translated by Barry Hudock. Revised edition. Collegeville, MN: Liturgical Press, 2013.

O'Collins, Gerald, with John Wilkins. *Lost in Translation: The English Language and the Catholic Mass.* Collegeville, MN: Liturgical Press, 2017.

2
SCRIPTURE

Ronald D. Witherup, PSS

Dei Verbum (*DV*), the Dogmatic Constitution on Divine Revelation, was the second draft document (or *schema*) presented to the council fathers for approbation in 1962 but ended up being one of the last documents approved. If the first text, *Sacrosanctum Concilium* (*SC*, Constitution on the Sacred Liturgy; approved 1963), passed with relative ease, this second one had a much more problematic and circuitous route to reach the finish line and become one of the most influential documents of Vatican II.

OVERVIEW

The first draft of this constitution got off to a bad start, as seen already in the draft's title. It was called *De Fontibus Revelationis* (On the Sources of Revelation), implying that there was more than one source of divine revelation. The intention had been to emphasize Scripture and Tradition as two sources by which God reveals himself. Immediately, however, numerous council fathers rose to oppose such an idea, pointing out that it was a misinterpretation of the teaching of the Council of Trent and contrary to the Church's traditional understanding of revelation, and not ecumenical enough. Trent had not conceived of Scripture and Tradition as two separate sources; rather Trent had spoken of one *source* of revelation (the gospel message) transmitted through two means. More importantly, ancient tradition viewed God's self-revelation as known through God's "deeds and words" throughout history (Acts 2:11) and not merely in propositional faith statements; this would ultimately find its way into the final text of *Dei Verbum* (§2).

With such vocal opposition, attempts to push the draft forward stalled. Neither side of the argument could achieve the required two-thirds majority to either pass or reject the draft. After a weeklong deadlock, which could have sabotaged the entire Council, only an unusual intervention by Pope John XXIII himself resolved the stalemate. He removed the document from the agenda and named a "mixed commission," intentionally headed by two opposing members of the Roman Curia, to gather a team of experts to redraft a new document on revelation. The process took all three remaining sessions of the Council and included thousands of emendations. Finally, on November 18, 1965, only weeks before the end of the Council, *Dei Verbum*, as the document was titled late in the process, was overwhelmingly approved by the council fathers and immediately promulgated by Pope Paul VI.

Content

The structure of the final text is itself instructive. A rather short document at only about three thousand words in the original Latin—compared to the other dogmatic constitution, *Lumen Gentium*, the Dogmatic Constitution on the Church, at some 23,800 words—it consists of a preface and six chapters that flow logically toward an evangelizing outlook. The first chapter discusses divine revelation itself and leads into the second, which lays out the various ways in which revelation is handed on. Only in the third chapter does the document turn explicitly to a discussion of the Sacred Scriptures, and then focuses the two subsequent chapters, respectively, on the Old and New Testaments. Finally, the sixth chapter broaches the question of the role of the Scriptures in the life of the Church. It concludes with a beautiful expression of the desire that the Scriptures be widely shared: "In this way, therefore, through the reading and study of the sacred books 'the word of God may spread rapidly and be glorified' (2 Thess 3:1) and the treasure of revelation, entrusted to the Church, may more and more fill the hearts of men" (§26).

Importantly, then, we should emphasize that *Dei Verbum*'s content is not merely about Scripture. The main theme is broader—divine revelation itself. Indeed, this document is the first in conciliar history to address the theme of divine revelation as a separate topic, apart from faith or other themes. The object of this orientation is to reinforce the importance of God's outreach to humanity. God freely takes this initiative. Receiving God's revelation by "hearing" and "proclaiming" God's word is to promote community or fellowship (Greek, *koinōnia*), first with the Triune God—Father, Son, and Holy Spirit—and also with all humanity. Revelation is thus first and foremost an invitation to a relationship with a loving God whose outreach is eternal.

General Strengths and Weaknesses

To evaluate *Dei Verbum* in the most general terms, I note three strengths and three weaknesses, some of which we will return to in our discussion in the next section.

The first and perhaps most striking strength is the emphasis on the *personal* nature of divine revelation. Whereas previous teachings on revelation had emphasized doctrinal and propositional aspects of divine revelation, *Dei Verbum* oriented the entire theme in terms of God's loving outreach to humanity. This is evident from the preface itself (§1) but also carries through to the end of the document (§26). Indeed, like bookends, the first and last paragraphs reinforce God's constant desire to make friends with all humanity and to invite us into relationship. This is quite different from asserting only doctrines or faith statements. While proclaiming doctrines and delineating the parameters of orthodox beliefs are important guideposts for authentic faith and help affirm Christian self-identity, emphasizing revelation as first and foremost God's outreach to humanity is more biblically sound and inviting.

A second strength is the use of scriptural quotations throughout the text. When we recognize that Catholics had, since the Reformation, tended to emphasize the sacraments in contrast to Protestant insistence on "Scripture alone" (*sola scriptura*), *Dei Verbum*'s use of the Scriptures and evident invitation to Catholics to embrace them is remarkable.

A third strength is the document's insistence on the *incarnational* dimension of revelation. This is not only seen in its reinforcement of the doctrine of the Incarnation—Jesus Christ as the *Logos*, the "Word made flesh" (§§4, 17)—but also in recognition that the Scriptures, analogously, are God's word in human words. Thus, there is an emphasis on the "deeds and words" of God throughout salvation history (§2), as well as a recognition that all the proper tools for understanding human communication must be used to understand God's word.

If these are some of the obvious strengths of *Dei Verbum*, there are also some evident weaknesses. The first is the treatment of the Old Testament in chapter 4. Early on, it was recognized as inadequate and superficial. This is even more remarkable given the Council's truly advanced teaching on

Judaism expressed in *Nostra Aetate*, the Declaration on the Relation of the Church to Non-Christian Religions (§4).

A second weakness is the lack of a more advanced and nuanced understanding of inspiration, the doctrine that God directly inspired the human authors by means of the Holy Spirit. Inspiration was affirmed but a more detailed explanation of it was lacking. This deficiency was noticeable, and Pope Benedict XVI in 2010 expressed the desire that this topic would be studied in more depth (*Verbum Domini* 19), which ultimately led to the Pontifical Biblical Commission's document, *The Inspiration and Truth of Sacred Scripture* (2014).

A third weakness is a lack of clarity regarding the main assertion that Scripture and Tradition form one means of divine revelation (§§9–10). The role of the magisterium (authoritative teaching office) was expressed almost as a third entity (§10), and the exact relationship between Scripture, Tradition, and the magisterium is left largely unexplained. This point remains important because some in the Church saw (and see) Tradition, narrowly defined as the magisterial teaching office, to be above Scripture rather than its equal. The constitution does not permit such a conclusion, since it literally declares, "This teaching office (*magisterium*) is not above the word of God, but serves (*ministrat*) it, teaching only what has been handed on, listening to it devoutly, guarding it scrupulously and explaining it faithfully in accord with a divine commission and with the help of the Holy Spirit" (§10).

This overview simply points to some obvious strengths and weaknesses that show the constitution was in the end a compromise document, in part owing to its long, contorted birth. This did not, however, impede *Dei Verbum*'s long-range impact on the Church's life.

Impact

From one perspective, the effect of *Dei Verbum* on the Church's life cannot be totally separated from the other fifteen documents of the Council. It is, for instance, one of the Council's four constitutions (*Sacrosanctum Concilium*, *Dei Verbum*, *Lumen Gentium*, and *Gaudium et Spes*), and one of only two "dogmatic constitutions," the other being *Lumen Gentium*. These constitutions have preeminent authority, in comparison to the remaining "decrees" and "declarations." Moreover, the two *dogmatic* constitutions are preeminent since they define two particularly critical parts of the faith—the nature of divine revelation and the nature of the Church. Despite it being composed late in the process and being promulgated only near the end of the Council, some experts have even proposed that the preface to *Dei Verbum* (§1) functions as a preface to the entire ecumenical Council, though others suggest *Sacrosanctum Concilium* as the guiding document.

Why? Four reasons justify such a prominent evaluation of *Dei Verbum*. First, the preface begins with the phrase "Hearing the word of God with reverence and proclaiming it with faith...." Such an expression emphasizes the Church's desire and duty to both "hear" the word of God—thus to receive it with care and to be subject to its authority—and proclaim it—thus to evangelize and to spread the truth of the word. The entire Council can be said to be an exercise in this evangelizing attitude. Secondly, using a citation from the First Letter of John (1:2–3), the preface also emphasizes that the invisible God of creation takes the initiative in reaching out to humanity in friendship through his own Son Jesus Christ, making this desire visible and concrete. Thirdly, the preface also notes that the constitution's teaching—and by extension the whole Council—is in continuity with prior Church teaching, especially Trent and Vatican I. It is a development of doctrine, not a rupture with the past. Finally, the preface cites the desire to promote the theological virtues: faith, leading to hope, leading to love—a perfect triad of the results of humbly accepting God's invitation to friendship.

In short, it is quite defensible to proclaim *Dei Verbum*'s teaching as both far-reaching and foundational.

Liturgy

Another area where *Dei Verbum*'s teaching was strongly felt was in conjunction with the liturgical reforms that quickly flowed from the first document to be promulgated, *Sacrosanctum Concilium*. This groundbreaking constitution asserted two primary truths that also found their way into *Dei Verbum*. The first affirmed the presence of the risen Christ when the word of God was read at liturgy: "He is present in His word, since it is He Himself who speaks when the holy scriptures are read in the Church" (§7). This is a powerful statement that likely startled many Catholics when they attended the revised Mass rites in the vernacular. The proclamation of the scriptural readings at Mass was just as important as the consecration of the bread and wine into the body and blood of Christ.

A second point reinforced this teaching later in the same constitution, when the unity of Word and Sacrament was affirmed: "The two parts which, in a certain sense, go to make up the Mass, namely, the liturgy of the word and the eucharistic liturgy, are so closely connected with each other that they form but one single act of worship" (§56). Such an affirmation of both/and—as in Word *and* Sacrament—is picked up in *Dei Verbum*, when it affirms that "the Church has always venerated the divine Scriptures just as she venerates the body of the Lord, since, especially in the sacred liturgy, she unceasingly receives and offers to the faithful the bread of life from the table both of God's word and of Christ's body" (§21).

In practical terms, both constitutions enabled Catholics to be exposed to a much wider swathe of biblical passages during Sunday Mass, which is the time when most Catholics attend church services. Utilizing three readings plus a psalm response—and from a much wider choice of Scriptures—enabled greater exposure of the Scriptures to Catholics. Hearing the readings in the vernacular, and hearing "homilies" (*DV* 24) rooted in the liturgical readings rather than "sermons" based on doctrinal or moral lessons also changed the way Catholics experienced the Scriptures.

Ecumenism

Vatican II, of course, was an ecumenical (from Greek, *oikoumenē*, "inhabited world") council, the twenty-first in Church history. It consequently constitutes the highest level of authoritative Church teaching. Pope John XXIII, however, had the vision of a council being "ecumenical" in a more expansive way. He invited non-Catholic observers to the Council, with the express desire to promote more dialogue and openness between various Christian denominations. This was an astounding move, given the four hundred years of separation between Catholics and Protestants, in particular, since the Reformation in the sixteenth century. Of course, the Council's landmark Decree on Ecumenism (*Unitatis Redintegratio*) and the controversial Declaration on Religious Freedom (*Dignitatis Humanae*) were both part of this openness. *Dei Verbum*, however, also contributed to this ecumenical fervor in two ways.

The first contribution is explicit. *Dei Verbum* called for Catholic scholars to participate, where possible, in cooperative ventures of Bible translation from the original languages (i.e., Hebrew, Greek, Aramaic) to make the Scriptures more accessible to everyone. "Easy access to Sacred Scripture should be provided for all the Christian faithful....And should the opportunity arise and the Church authorities approve, if these translations are produced in cooperation with the separated brethren as well, all Christians will be able to use them" (§22; see also §25). This quickly became a reality, as several international and ecumenical translations went on to be produced, one of the most recent being the New Revised Standard Version (1989). Moreover, ecumenical dialogues flourished in which the ecumenical study of important biblical passages was central (e.g., *Peter in the New Testament* [1973] and *Mary in the New Testament* [1978], among others).

The second aspect is more implicit. Although *Dei Verbum* has little to say explicitly about methods in biblical studies, it nevertheless encouraged Catholic biblical scholars to use all appropriate means to foster expert study of the Sacred Scriptures (§12). "Catholic exegetes then and other students of sacred theology, working diligently together and using appropriate means, should devote their energies, under the watchful care of the sacred teaching office of the Church, to an exploration and exposition of the divine writings" (§23). This is a cautious statement and recalls the magisterial role of oversight, yet it repeated Pope Pius XII's groundbreaking encouragement of modern, scientific biblical study by Catholic scholars promoted in his farsighted encyclical *Divino Afflante Spiritu* (1943). In fact, already in the years leading up to the Council and during it, Catholic scholars had been implementing this vision by adopting modern scientific exegetical methods, getting advance degrees, and participating fruitfully in ecumenical dialogues. Catholic biblical scholarship began to flourish after the Council, and names like Raymond E. Brown, Joseph A. Fitzmyer, and Roland E. Murphy—the three main editors of the *Jerome Biblical Commentary* (1968) and its successor the *New Jerome Biblical Commentary* (1990)—among others, became identified with solid Catholic biblical scholarship on a par with non-Catholic experts. *Dei Verbum*, in essence, signaled that Catholic biblical scholarship had come of age.

Laity and the Bible

Even though many Catholic laity likely never read this groundbreaking conciliar document, they were nonetheless beneficiaries of its revitalizing vision of renewing the role of Scripture in the Church's life. This was evident in the multiple popular publications that began to appear, the proliferation of Bible study programs, conferences, and workshops that grew, and in the attempts to make Sunday homilies more biblical through the expanded readings used at Sunday Mass. It was as if *Dei Verbum* had allowed a latent burning passion for the word of God to burst forth, something I personally experienced as a seminarian attending in-depth Scripture courses that enhanced my spiritual and formal understanding of the Bible. The Council's encouragement of lay involvement in the faith, expressed in the Decree on the Apostolate of the Laity (*Apostolicam Actuositatem*, 1965) was itself based on the testimony of the Scriptures in the early Church (§1).

These are but a few of the ways *Dei Verbum* helped transform the Church's life after the Council. We now turn to further developments.

OTHER CHURCH DOCUMENTS AND ISSUES FOR THE FUTURE

One way to judge the impact of *Dei Verbum* is to see its influence in subsequent official documents. Despite being the foundational authoritative document for a Catholic approach to the Bible, it was not the end of the line. Since the *living tradition* of the Church (*DV* 8) always continues to develop, it is not surprising that *Dei Verbum* provided the springboard for subsequent Church teaching, which has gone on to nuance and develop its perspective. We will examine several illustrations.

The first is the *Catechism of the Catholic Church* (*CCC*, 2nd ed., 1994). It features many citations from *Dei Verbum* in the section on Sacred Scripture (§§101–41). Two highlights are worth noting because they address neuralgic issues. One is the quotation of *Dei Verbum* which explained that the concept of inspiration of Scripture was not to be equated with "inerrancy," a term the constitution intentionally avoided. Instead, the constitution affirmed that "the books of Scripture must be acknowledged as teaching solidly, faithfully and *without error* that truth which God wanted put into sacred writings *for the sake of salvation*" (§11; *CCC* 107). The phrasing is an implicit acknowledgment that the Bible's religious message, for salvation, is not to be confused with historical or scientific meanings. The second highlight was the acknowledgment that the formation of the four Gospels happened through a complex and lengthy process in three stages: the life and teaching of Jesus, the oral traditions of those who preached the gospel, and the traditions collected, written, and edited by the evangelists (*DV* 19; *CCC* 126). Such a formulation precludes the idea that the Gospels are literal, factual accounts of every detail of the ministry of Jesus.

In the decades following the Council, many other developments concerning the Scriptures also appeared. The Pontifical Biblical Commission continued to do its careful research and produced numerous documents concerning such diverse topics as Christology (1984), the interpretation of the Bible in the Church (1993), the Jewish people and their Scriptures (2002), the Bible and morality (2008), and the inspiration and truth of Sacred Scripture (2014). These ongoing studies add to the unique resources for Catholics to comprehend the Bible and provide sure guidance on many controversial topics.

Popes have also contributed to a Catholic understanding of the Scriptures through numerous teachings. Most importantly, Benedict XVI—who as Joseph Ratzinger was a *peritus* (expert consultor) at the Council and was involved in the production of *Dei Verbum*—promulgated *Verbum Domini* (2010), an apostolic exhortation that grew out of a 2008 worldwide synod on the word of God. Citations from *Dei Verbum* are widely scattered in various parts of the exhortation, including key passages, underlining the importance of the constitution for all subsequent Catholic exploration of Scripture.

Pope Francis has also utilized the Scriptures in multiple ways, even apart from his Wednesday general audiences and many of his homilies and allocutions. His first apostolic exhortation, *Evangelii Gaudium* (*EG*, 2013), while not explicitly on the Scriptures, exhorted Catholics to engage them and use them for proclaiming the authenticity of the gospel message. The lengthy section on the role of the homily in Sunday Mass (*EG* 135–44) is a masterful treatment of how modern preachers should engage the word of God and make it more understandable, an explicit affirmation of *Dei Verbum*'s desire that the word be spread far and wide (*DV* 21–26).

More recently, Pope Francis tried to rekindle Catholic interest in Scripture—an express purpose of *Dei Verbum*, which asserted the Scriptures as the "soul of sacred theology" (§24)—by establishing the third Sunday of the liturgical year as a "Sunday of the Word of God," proclaimed in his apostolic letter *Aperuit Illis* (2019).

Dei Verbum, as a dogmatic constitution, will obviously continue to guide the Church on the question of revelation even as new insights emerge under the guidance of the Holy Spirit. As seminal a text as *Dei Verbum* is, there is room for more advancement in our knowledge and application of the Sacred Scriptures and Tradition as the privileged means of divine revelation. Without being exhaustive or pretending to forecast the future, I suggest five areas that will need further work.

First, there is still debate among scholars about the distinctive features of a Catholic approach to Scripture. Some feel that the modern scientific study of the holy writ has watered down its spiritual or theological message. Some even propose prescientific patristic and medieval interpretation as the most fruitful way to interpret Scripture. Others see the development of many kinds of postmodern methodologies as warped and ideologically driven. These kinds of issues will need to be addressed by those who want seriously to interpret the Bible faithfully. Given the fact that there is no one method of Bible study that characterizes Catholic exegesis (as the Pontifical Biblical Commission affirmed in their 1993 text, *The Interpretation of the Bible in the Church*), questions of how to appropriate and use methods will pose challenges for Catholic scholars for years to come.

A second area remains how best to read the Scriptures with a sensitivity to other faiths. Often Catholics naively, and perhaps unknowingly, offend Jewish sensitivities, for example, by wrongly opposing Jesus and the Pharisees. Modern scholarship has more clearly shown that this is a misreading of the New Testament and does not do justice to the role of the Pharisees in preserving Judaism after the destruction of Jerusalem by the Romans in AD 70. Even the appreciation of the Old Testament in *Dei Verbum*, as mentioned above, is inadequate. There is still a widespread misunderstanding that the God of the Old Testament is different from the God of the New, something which *Dei Verbum* contradicts (§16), and which the Biblical Commission's document *The Jewish People and Their Sacred Scriptures in the Christian Bible* (2002) also debunks.

Third, our modern age has seen increasing divisions in humanity, in nations, in politics, and even in the Church. Coping with a pluralistic and multicultural world has not been easy. Prejudices and even violent intolerance have sharply increased since the turn of the third millennium, and the Scriptures continually are invoked to justify—usually improperly—intolerant actions. The danger is always falling into the trap of "proof texting," wrongly using Scripture to justify one position or another. While the conciliar documents employ this same method from time to time, usually the use of scriptural citations leans more toward illustration rather than proving a point. Catholics are not immune to misreading and misusing Scripture, such as to justify the death penalty, condemn homosexuals, dismiss immigrants, or tout a "gospel of prosperity." The Church must still grapple with how to invite Catholics to read Scripture more responsibly, and to avoid any tendency toward biblical fundamentalism.

A fourth area concerns the great shifts we have seen in modern technological advancement. With the increased use of social media, young people especially are more influenced by images, videos, and short sound bites than by printed text. The fact is that most millennials and those of so-called Generation Z do not read the way previous generations did. What does this mean for a faith devoted to the word? The authors of *Dei Verbum*, of course, could never have foreseen the situation as it exists today. But ultimately, the Church needs to wrestle with this changing reality in a world where traditional books and texts no longer hold a strong appeal to many people.

Finally, a fifth area relates to *Dei Verbum*'s great insistence on the "incarnational principle." This was truly one of the great insights of the constitution, but it remains one that many Catholics find hard to implement. It is difficult to comprehend how the Scriptures are at one and the same time both God's word—God is the true "author"—and human words, in which real human authors used the language of their era to express the divine message (as affirmed in §11). *Dei Verbum* uses the analogy of the Incarnation (§13)—that God became human—to speak of this extraordinary relationship, and it acknowledges that it is a "mystery," a biblical term reemployed in the constitution (§§2, 17) and other documents of the Council (*SC* 47; *LG* 3). Yet, there is still a tendency to collapse the two. The divine element too often subsumes the human, and thus the word is misapplied and misunderstood while invoking "divine" authority.

In the end, if there is still much that can be done to implement *Dei Verbum* more profoundly, we can be grateful that this revolutionary document placed the Church's appreciation of divine revelation on a firm footing.

FOR FURTHER READING

Montague, George T. *Understanding the Bible: A Basic Introduction to Biblical Interpretation*. Revised and expanded ed. Mahwah, NJ: Paulist Press, 2007.

Okoye, James Chukwuma. *Scripture in the Church: The Synod on the Word of God*. Collegeville, MN: Liturgical Press, 2011.

Witherup, Ronald D. *Scripture: Dei Verbum*. Rediscovering Vatican II. Mahwah, NJ: Paulist Press, 2006.

———. *The Word of God at Vatican II: Exploring* Dei Verbum. Collegeville, MN: Liturgical Press, 2014.

3

THE CHURCH

Kristin Colberg

Vatican II was a council about the Church. This might not seem like a bold statement, but it is. Certainly, all councils deal with the Church on some level, yet no other council directed its focus in the same way. Treating the Church as a discrete topic is a relatively recent development in the theological tradition, appearing most frequently following the Protestant Reformation as differing visions of the Church and its authority emerged. Only at Vatican II's immediate predecessor, Vatican I (1869–70), did a council dedicate an explicit document to ecclesiology. Vatican II's decision to center its reflections on the nature and mission of the Church was not merely a content choice; rather it signaled the uniqueness of this gathering and its desire to engage modern concerns. Placing the Church at the center of the Council impacted all of Vatican II's deliberations and continues to shape our understanding and experience of the Church today.

Throughout Christian history, councils typically gathered (to borrow a phrase from spy novelist Tom Clancy) to respond to a "clear and present danger." Accordingly, these gatherings generally operated in a defensive mode seeking to distance the Church from individuals, groups, or practices that the Council or its leaders perceived as threatening. In this way, councils generally sought to stop specific theological conversations and restore order. To that end, councils often use legalistic language that establishes the Church's positions as clear, timeless, and unassailable. John XXIII envisioned a different approach. Rather than assembling the bishops to define and potentially stop certain conversations, he desired a gathering that would start conversations both within the Church as well as between the Church and the world. He hoped that this gathering would lead the Church in a process of *aggiornamento*, or updating, which would be guided, in part, by a *ressourcement*, or return to the sources, whereby the community could consider its own ancient tradition as a source for renewing itself to meet contemporary needs.

Many were excited about John XXIII's vision, but it also raised logistical problems. When a council meets in a defensive mode, the gathering's purpose is typically clear: deal with a given threat. Since Vatican II gathered under drastically different conditions, the council fathers struggled to decide exactly where to start, what to do, and how to organize their work. Sensing that the gathering needed a clear theme to provide direction and unity to its deliberations, several key figures involved in developing the Council's agenda sought to center its focus on the Church.

Two primary reasons motivated this choice. First, many of the bishops understood that while the authority of the Church and its place in society were taken for granted in past centuries, many people in the modern world not only doubted ecclesial authority but rejected it outright; therefore, for the Church to speak as a compelling voice in society, the Council needed to demonstrate its ability to speak meaningfully to contemporary issues. Second, Vatican I (1869–70) famously defined the authority of the pope in clear and strong terms.

However, before the bishops could consider other complementary aspects of the Church's nature, and thus set its treatment of the pope within an appropriate context, the Council was suspended due to the outbreak of the Franco-Prussian War. As a result, Vatican I offered an incomplete and one-sided presentation of the Church that caused significant problems both theologically and practically. Therefore, to meet the current needs and engage silences from the past, those planning Vatican II chose the Church as the Council's primary theme.

While all Vatican II's documents deal with the Church, two of the four major constitutions take this topic as their main focus: The Dogmatic Constitution on the Church (*Lumen Gentium* [*LG*]) and the Pastoral Constitution on the Church in the Modern World (*Gaudium et Spes* [*GS*]). Scholars note that *Lumen Gentium* treats the Church *ad intra*, meaning that it deals with matters internal to the Church itself, and *Gaudium et Spes* treats the Church *ad extra*, regarding how it relates to the rest of the world. While we cannot fully separate the Church's "internal" and "external" aspects, this is generally a helpful way to approach the aims and content of these documents.

OUTLINE

Lumen Gentium comprises eight chapters, the order of which is significant. The first chapter, "The Mystery of the Church," represents one of the greatest breakthroughs of the Council. Rather than presenting the Church in a defensive mode characterized by legal definitions and a focus on visible structures, *Lumen Gentium* emphasizes the Church's nature as a mystery (*mystērion* in Greek). Today, we usually understand the word mystery to mean something that is unknown or to signify a lack of knowledge, but in the New Testament, and particularly Paul's letters, this term was used to convey a reality with endless depths. By identifying the Church as a mystery, Vatican II signals that no definition can capture the reality of the Church and that, instead, its signification requires a variety of images and metaphors. *Lumen Gentium*'s first chapter refers to the Church as a sacrament, a word whose roots are closely associated with mystery. Identifying the Church as a sacrament affirms the importance of the Church's visible structures but highlights that these structures exist to point us to the deeper, invisible reality of God's presence in the world. The nature of the Church as a mystery and a sacrament finds expression in the constitution's opening proclamation: "Christ is the Light of nations" (*Lumen* = light, *Gentium* = nations). Consequently, *Lumen Gentium* breaks from the juridical models of recent decades to highlight that the Church is not an ultimate reality or end in itself; rather, as the preeminent sacrament or sign, it exists to point beyond itself to Christ.

Another advance comes in *Lumen Gentium*'s second chapter, "The People of God." The chapter teaches that God reveals God's self, through the Holy Spirit, to the whole body of the faithful and, accordingly, the entire people of God possess an innate sense of the faith, making them co-responsible for the Church. Thereby, through baptism, the whole Christian faithful are equal in dignity and called to a common priesthood (*LG* 10). These affirmations signal critical achievements in themselves, but their meaning gains greater significance by the fact that they precede the discussion of the hierarchy in *Lumen Gentium*'s third chapter. Considering the dignity of all the baptized members of the people of God ahead of the authority of the hierarchy underscores the reality that what unites Christians is more important than what distinguishes them. In other words, the fact that Kristin Colberg and the pope share a common baptism and membership in the body of Christ is more fundamental than the fact that each plays a different role in the body.

Vatican II's choice to ground the Church primarily in baptism rather than in hierarchy transformed people's understanding of the ecclesial community and their role within it. This position establishes the basic methodology of the Council: it is an act of *ressourcement* in that it retrieves the centrality of baptism as key to the Church's identity and, in doing so, it helps the Church achieve much-needed *aggiornamento* by fueling contemporary efforts to diversify ecclesial leadership, advance Christian unity, and renew notions of authority. Furthermore, the significance of the ordering of these chapters provides an example of the way that the Council's style (*how* it teaches) is critical to understanding its meaning (*what* it teaches). The third chapter of *Lumen Gentium* on the hierarchy is important because it is "ground zero" for the Council's efforts to address Vatican I's silences. It begins by affirming Vatican I's teaching on the pope and then proceeds to affirm the authority of the bishop and the college of bishops (*LG* 18). In doing so, it seeks to address some of the one-sidedness of Vatican I's presentation of the Church. Achieving this balance is not merely a technical matter, it advances critical questions about how a global Church balances unity and diversity.

The five remaining chapters of *Lumen Gentium* treat other vital aspects of the Church's identity, exploring how the mystery of the Church and the vocation of the people of God are lived out in the world. Chapters 4 through 7 speak of a universal call to holiness and the pilgrim nature of the Church; they also treat the roles of the laity and the clergy. Chapter 8 on Mary deserves special mention. This chapter passed with the closest vote at the Council (1,114 to 1,074). The controversy was not about the content of the chapter, but its placement. Since a primary goal of Vatican II was to present the Church's identity, there was wide agreement that Mary should receive significant treatment. Some bishops felt that Mary's role was so important that it warranted its own chapter while others worried that such a move would undermine ecumenical progress. The decision to emphasize Mary as the "Mother of the Church" and include this material as the final chapter in *Lumen Gentium* illustrates an act of "doing" ecumenism. It is "doing" ecumenism because rather than merely affirming the importance of Christian unity, it seeks to advance the cause through ecumenical sensitivity and creating avenues for dialogue. Here, again, we see a clear example of the fact that Vatican II's style (*how* it teaches) is critical to understanding its content (*what* it teaches).

A NEW VISION AND APPROACH

Vatican II's vision of the Church is also powerfully conveyed in *Gaudium et Spes*. In this document, the focus shifts to the Church's expression of its identity through its engagement with the world. *Gaudium et Spes* constitutes a unique text within an already unique council. A text like this was largely unimaginable before Vatican II began; it represents the fruit of the world's bishops coming together to deliberate about "the joys and the hopes, the griefs and the anxieties" of the modern world (*GS* 1). *Gaudium et Spes* begins by linking itself to *Lumen Gentium*. It begins: "Hence this Second Vatican Council, having probed more profoundly into the mystery of the Church, now addresses itself without hesitation, not only to the sons of the Church and to all who invoke the name of Christ, but to the whole of humanity. For the Council yearns to explain to everyone how it conceives of the presence and activity of the Church in the world of today" (*GS* 2). Immediately, we see one of the text's innovative features: dialogical tone. *Gaudium et Spes* does not merely state the importance of dialogue (*what* it teaches); it initiates a dialogue (*how* it teaches). Furthermore, its invitation addresses not only Christians but "the whole of humanity."

To engage this wide audience, *Gaudium et Spes* employed the strategy of raising questions. Paragraph 10 asks, "What is man? What is this sense of sorrow, of evil, of death, which continues to exist despite so much progress? What purpose have these victories purchased at so high a cost? What can man offer to society, what can he expect from it? What follows this earthly life?" The Council did not seek to "answer" these questions; rather, it sought to create common ground from which to begin and continue conversations. Previous councils often avoided posing questions without supplying ready responses since the lack of a definitive answer could give the impression that the Church was unauthoritative or unreliable. Vatican II did not share the same fear. Instead, it understood the Church as a fellow pilgrim in the world that did not possess every solution, but that did have the truth of the gospel to share with all humanity.

To achieve its goals, *Gaudium et Spes* adopts a groundbreaking starting point. Traditionally, conciliar texts began by reflecting on Scripture, Christ, or magisterial teaching. Starting from an area of strength or expertise made sense given that previous councils sought to prove a point and conclude a conversation. Vatican II, however, realized that for a large portion of the modern world, these traditional starting points were "nonstarters" and would fail to engage "the whole of humanity." Thus, *Gaudium et Spes* opted to begin with something to which all its readers had access: human experience. The council fathers realized that for the Church to speak meaningfully in the contemporary context it had to demonstrate that it recognized the struggles, goals, and longings of people in the mid-twentieth century. Paragraph 4 of *Gaudium et Spes* tries to show such awareness:

> Never has the human race enjoyed such an abundance of wealth, resources and economic power, and yet a huge proportion of the world's citizens are still tormented by hunger and poverty, while countless numbers suffer from total illiteracy. Never before has man had so keen an understanding of freedom, yet at the same time new forms of social and psychological slavery make their appearance. Although the world of today has a very vivid awareness of its unity and of how one man depends on another in needful solidarity, it is most grievously torn into opposing camps by conflicting forces....Finally, man painstakingly searches for a better world, without a corresponding spiritual advancement. (*GS* 4)

The Council's ability to read the "signs of the times" and willingness to engage concrete issues presented the Church in a new light, not as an institution focused on timeless truths but as a community in the world affected by history and engaged with humanity's concerns.

At its heart, *Gaudium et Spes* asks the question: What does the Church have to offer the modern world? The response that the document offers centers largely on the lamented lack of a "corresponding spiritual advancement" mentioned in the passage above. Individuals, institutions, and nations often see progress and value only in terms of economic, technological, or political advancement, and they fail to attend to the spiritual dimension of human existence. *Gaudium et Spes* contends that such views fail to appreciate that human beings are spiritual creatures whose nature exceeds the limitations of empirical observation and the sum of their parts. Human beings possess a transcendent dimension that propels them to reach beyond themselves and beyond the material realm in a quest to find meaning and wholeness. The modern world's tendency toward a myopic focus on material gains "without a parallel spiritual advancement" leaves contemporary individuals feeling lost, homeless, fragmented, and without a way of understanding their own existence. Thus, *Gaudium et Spes* teaches that the Church has something essential to offer the modern world: a more adequate understanding of what it means to be human and wisdom about how to live a more fully human existence.

While Vatican II explored the nature and mission of the Church, it did not seek to introduce new doctrine on this topic. Instead, it sought a renewal of the Church itself, a renewal that would allow the Church to live out its identity more authentically. To achieve this, the Council did not approach the Church as a series of truths to be known, but as a mystery to be experienced and lived. We have seen in the decades since the Council that this renewal of the Church continues. One of the most famous Catholic theologians of the twentieth century, Karl Rahner, SJ, famously stated that councils are always both an end and a beginning. They are an end because their deliberations allow the Church to arrive at decisions that bring closure to some questions and they are a beginning because, in clarifying specific issues, councils raise new questions and possibilities. While Rahner's observation applies to all councils, it is especially true of Vatican II. It is not an exaggeration to say that Vatican II's impact on the Church has been so profound that all conversations about the Church today have ties to the Council's documents. While it is not possible to map out all the ways that Vatican II was a beginning, here we will explore two prominent streams of conversation following the Council: authority and dialogue.

AUTHORITY AND DIALOGUE

Vatican II's teachings catalyzed conversations about authority on every level of the Church's life. On one level, the Council launched further discussions about the relationship between the pope and the bishops. While Vatican II addressed some of the silences of Vatican I by affirming that the pope and his brother bishops share responsibility in governing the Church, a principle known as episcopal collegiality, it did not resolve some of the complex questions about *how* they share authority. People often characterize episcopal collegiality as a potentially "boring" subject akin to examining an organizational flowchart. However, when we examine the role of the bishops in relation to the pope, in essence, we probe the vital balance between unity and diversity in the Church. The amount of authority or autonomy of a local bishop or an episcopal conference determines the extent to which local churches can express their experience of Christ in distinctive ways that reflect their context. Such diverse expressions give the Church vibrancy and relevance around the world, yet this diversity needs to be held in healthy tension with expressions of faith that unite the global Church and keep it rooted in its tradition, tasks critically belonging to the papal primacy. This topic has been of particular importance to Pope Francis who noted in *Evangelii Gaudium* (*EG*) that Vatican II's desire to achieve a greater understanding of the authority of bishops working together in episcopal conferences "has not been fully realized" and called for greater elaboration on this topic. Furthermore, he pointed to the problem of not properly understanding the balance of authority between the pope and the bishops by stating that "excessive centralization, rather than proving helpful, complicates the Church's life and her missionary outreach" (*EG* 32). Therefore, discussions about the way that the pope and the bishops share authority are not esoteric considerations about "Who does what when?"; they constitute vital conversations for a global Church that seeks to maintain its identity *and* express itself meaningfully in an endless variety of contexts.

Conversations about authority in the Church after Vatican II have also considered the role of the laity. The question of shared authority between bishops and the pope at the Council led to questions about other ways that authority could be shared in the Church, among the whole people of God. *Lumen Gentium*'s emphasis on baptismal dignity and other conciliar teachings such as *Sacrosanctum Concilium*'s (*SC*) call for full, conscious, and active participation in the liturgy (*SC* 41), initiated significant shifts in the laity's self-understanding, including their responsibility for lay ecclesial ministry, an area of explosive growth over the last half century. Studies show that, in the United States, there are now more lay ecclesial ministers than ordained ministers in the Catholic Church. This shift has occasioned considerable reflection on the nature of ministry and the role of the hierarchy as a vital yet not singular source of leadership in the Church. An example of this type of reflection exists in the document "Co-Workers in the Vineyard of the Lord" by the United States Conference of Catholic Bishops, which describes and explores the reality of lay ecclesial ministry. This text represented a significant advance when it came out almost twenty years ago and continues to provide a foundation for ongoing efforts to understand the entire people of God as co-responsible coworkers who are all called and sent to spread the gospel through words and deeds. Conversations about leadership and co-responsibility have generated critical discussions about the extent to which the Church is welcoming of all people and their gifts. Interestingly, while Vatican II's view of the Church has energized many members of the laity who have responded affirmatively to the call to ministerial leadership, the years after the Council have also seen a steep decline in Mass attendance and the reception of other sacraments in the

United States and Europe. Scholars speculate about whether Vatican II's shift away from legislative language and goals catalyzed a shift among the faithful from perceiving regular Mass attendance as a primary way of living out their faith. A critical concern in the decades since the Council has been the loss of youth and young adults who increasingly feel a distance from the institutional Church. The situation has surfaced questions about how the transformative vision of authority offered by Vatican II can renew the Church's structures and empower a new generation of leaders.

A second stream of conversations inaugurated by Vatican II has focused on the Church's dialogues with other Christians, members of other religious traditions, and with the secular realm. A focal point in these discussions has been the relationship between dialogue and proclamation. Vatican II emphasized the importance of dialogue as a "two-way street," yet in the years since the Council, some have argued that this emphasis on dialogue as a mutual conversation and search for common ground can jeopardize the imperative to proclaim boldly the truth of the gospel. In honor of the twenty-fifth anniversary of *Nostra Aetate*, the Pontifical Council for Interreligious Dialogue explored questions related to interreligious exchange in an important document entitled "Dialogue and Proclamation." Reflecting on the Council's achievements and the need to constantly discern effective means of evangelization, this text seeks to hold proclamation and dialogue together as a both/and rather than an either/or. These debates over dialogue, like those about authority, surface questions about the role of diversity and inculturation in the Church. Does embracing too much diversity or certain types of diversity run the risk of fragmenting the Church or separating the Church from its tradition? Following Vatican II, many have concluded that dialogue and exchange with the world cannot exist only on the level of ideas; it must include action, particularly actions oriented toward justice. People observe that while Vatican II initially expressed a commitment to focusing on the poor and a desire to become a Church for the poor, this vision did not come to full expression.

Shortly after the Council, for example, the bishops of the Latin American and Caribbean Episcopal Council (CELAM) committed themselves to addressing this conciliar inadequacy. Accordingly, since Vatican II, we have seen the rise of liberation theologies seeking to liberate people from the conditions that inhibit the full realization of their human dignity. Vatican II's affirmations that the Church is a sacrament, and that people are spiritual and temporal, remind the Church not to concern itself only with people's spiritual well-being and not to remain only in the realm of ideas, but to commit itself to working for justice and the flourishing of individuals as whole persons. CELAM has helped the whole Church better understand key aspects of Vatican II's ecclesial vision. Taking the Council's teaching on the people of God as a key starting point, CELAM has been a leader in efforts to invert pyramidal visions of the Church such that the top, typically understood as the hierarchy, is now located beneath the base so that all the people of God are called to listen to one another, and authority is understood as service. As a result, it has worked to develop vibrant methods of decision-making, faith sharing, and accompaniment of those on the margins on the local level. The impact of these developments is especially pronounced given that they helped shape Jorge Mario Bergoglio whose ministry as Pope Francis reflects many of these commitments.

CONCLUSION

As we read the signs of the times today and look to the future, it appears that our world, as at the time of Vatican II, stands at the threshold of a new era. Faced with seismic shifts and uncertainty, the Church must respond to significant challenges, such as systemic violations of human rights, environmental degradation, economic inequality, rapid declines in religious affiliation and religious vocations in many places around the world, and calls for greater inclusion in the Church. Following the model pioneered by John XXIII and Vatican II, Pope Francis opted not to mount a defensive response to these challenges, but to address the needs of the moment by promoting conversation.

To meet the needs of today and tomorrow, the Church has embarked on a journey toward greater synodality. Pope Francis speaks of synodality as the process of creating a "listening church," one that seeks radical openness, inclusion, and a desire for dialogue. Synodality is, in many ways, an effort to further unpack and implement the theology of Vatican II, particularly its understanding of the Church. As we have seen, Vatican II powerfully affirms that the people of God are not passive subjects. They are active agents who receive and transmit the word of God and, as such, are co-responsible for the Church's mission. While this theology is clearly expressed in Vatican II's documents, it remains to be fully realized in all the Church's structures, communicative dynamics, and actions. In pursuing greater synodality, Francis asked: What would the Church look like if it lived out the ecclesiology of Vatican II? To discern an answer, he asked every parish in the world to hold listening sessions where all were invited to speak. At the heart of these listening sessions were two basic questions: What is the Holy Spirit calling the Church to in the current moment? And how can the Church best walk together in response to that call? Francis encouraged everyone to speak freely (*parrhesia*) and stated that no topics were out of bounds. It is hard to imagine a more radical effort on the Church's part to initiate rather than end conversations.

FOR FURTHER READING

Colberg, Kristin. *Vatican I and Vatican II: Councils in the Living Tradition*. Collegeville, MN: Liturgical Press, 2016.

Gaillardetz, Richard. *The Church in the Making: Lumen Gentium, Christus Dominus, Orientalium Ecclesiarum*. Mahwah, NJ: Paulist Press, 2006.

Hahnenberg, Edward P. *A Concise Guide to the Documents of Vatican II*. Cincinnati, OH: St. Anthony Messenger Press, 2007.

Ilo, Stan Chu. *A Poor and Merciful Church: The Illuminative Ecclesiology of Pope Francis*. Maryknoll, NY: Orbis, 2018.

Lakeland, Paul. *A Council That Will Never End: Lumen Gentium and the Church Today*. Collegeville, MN: Liturgical Press, 2013.

O'Malley, John W. *What Happened at Vatican II*. Cambridge: Harvard University Press, 2010.

Rush, Ormond. *The Vision of Vatican II: Its Fundamental Principles*. Collegeville, MN: Liturgical Press, 2019.

Sullivan, Maureen. *The Road to Vatican II: Key Changes in Theology*. Mahwah, NJ: Paulist Press, 2007.

4

RELIGIOUS LIFE, BISHOPS, PRIESTS, AND DEACONS

William T. Ditewig

Our task is to review some highlights from the Second Vatican Council about what we may call the "official" ministries in the Church. This includes those women and men who live out the evangelical counsels (poverty, chastity, and obedience) in consecrated religious life, as well as the ordained vocations of bishops, priests, and deacons. As we embark on this wide-ranging journey, we must keep two things in mind.

First, we should remember that when entering into the event that was Vatican II, we have landed *in medias res*, in the middle of things. The work of the bishops at the Second Vatican Council did not emerge from a vacuum. In every case, theologians, church officials, religious leaders, and pastors had been discussing and debating many of these issues for decades. Take just one example: the diaconate. How to renew a standing diaconate had been the subject of speculation and research since early in the nineteenth century, with contemporary interest exploding in the aftermath of the Second World War. The Second Vatican Council can thus be seen as taking up the various threads of these debates, affirming the principles necessary for their contemporary resolution, and attempting to integrate them into a systematic whole. To understand any one issue, we must first see how it fits into the larger mosaic of ecclesial reform and renewal.

Second, we should consider the documents of the Council in two ways. Naturally, they provide the foundations and principles of renewal developed by the council fathers. But they also serve as launch pads for subsequent magisterial documents and events. For example, in addition to several significant postconciliar papal documents on consecrated life, changes were made to the Code of Canon Law, and in 1994, St. John Paul II convened a General Synod on "The Consecrated Life and Its Role in the Church and in the World."

We turn our attention to these ministries through the lens of selected Council documents. All ministry—lay, professed religious, or ordained—takes place within the framework and on the foundation of the Church. As seen in chapter 3, the dogmatic nature and pastoral mission of the Church are addressed by two Council constitutions: the Dogmatic Constitution on the Church, *Lumen Gentium* (*LG*), and the Pastoral Constitution on the Church in the Modern World, *Gaudium et Spes* (*GS*). *Lumen Gentium* is the starting point for any discussion of ministry in the Church. The subsequent decrees are built on that foundation.

THE FOUNDATION OF ALL MINISTRY

For Catholic Christians, everything begins with baptism. Baptism not only immerses us into the life of the Trinity, but it also serves as our first call to ministry. During the rite of baptism, the deacon or priest anoints the newly baptized with sacred chrism and reminds them that God has freed them from sin, given them a new birth by water and the Holy Spirit, and welcomed them into his holy people. But the prayer continues, "[God] now anoints you with the chrism of salvation. As Christ was anointed Priest, Prophet, and King, so may you live always as a member of his body, sharing everlasting life." In the Old Testament, Jewish priests, prophets, and kings were anointed with sacred oil to give them strength to carry out their God-given tasks. In Christ, we find this tradition perfected. Through baptism, all the faithful, regardless of their state of life, are called to perfection in holiness and to participate in those ministries, regardless of their state of life. It is on this common priesthood of the faithful, the foundation of ministry, that we now turn to the specialized ministries within the Church.

CONSECRATED LIFE: *PERFECTAE CARITATIS*

If you ask many Catholics in the United States about their understanding of the Church of the 1950s, you will hear how healthy the Church seemed, with convents overflowing with sisters, seminaries full of candidates for the priesthood, and parishes packed with the faithful. Larger parishes often had their own schools fully staffed by the sisters, and the rectory housed two or three full-time priests.

The worldwide reality was different. Vocations to religious life had been declining since the end of the Second World War. This was especially true in Europe. The horrors of two world wars, economic collapse, the Holocaust, the emergence of nuclear arms, and the Cold War, caused church leaders and theologians to reexamine the nature of the Church and the role of the laity in the Church. Laity, and in some cases, lay religious institutes were formed that did not require their members to make vows of poverty, chastity, and obedience. There were two World Congresses for the Lay Apostolate (in 1951 and 1957). At the same time, the leadership of various religious congregations realized that changes were needed if religious life were to continue to serve the emerging needs of people in the contemporary world. More and more religious pursued higher education, and there were frequent conferences on possible reforms. Pope Pius XII often exhorted religious to find new ways of serving.

Concurrently, through the work of theologians such as Yves Congar, the laity of the Church were rediscovering the significance of their baptismal identity. To seek holiness and to exercise one's baptismal responsibilities, one did not have to make solemn and perpetual vows of poverty, chastity, and obedience. While this insight is an important one that will be covered in chapter 7, it also contributed to a steady erosion of vowed and ordained vocations throughout the 1940s and 1950s. The question for the Council would be how to preserve the charisms and blessings of consecrated life, while concurrently developing the theology of the laity and a universal call to perfection in holiness, despite one's state in life.

During the Council

The first draft of a document on consecrated life was titled "On the States of Acquiring Perfection." The bishops quickly rejected this approach, and the final document reveals the growth in the bishops' understanding: "The Decree on the Up-to-Date Renewal of Religious Life." The history of *Perfectae Caritatis* (*PC*) is complex; we will focus on two issues.

First, prior to the Council, a vocation to religious life was described in terms of living the evangelical counsels of chastity, poverty, and obedience to seek perfection of personal holiness. But the Council moved away from the notion that one group of Christians could be "more perfect" than another. Rather, all the baptized are to seek perfection in holiness, regardless of their state of life. After discussing the universal call to perfect holiness, the council fathers wrote in *Lumen Gentium* that "from the point of view of the divine and hierarchical structure of the Church, the religious state of life is not an intermediate state between the clerical and lay states. But, rather, the faithful of Christ are called by God from both these states of life so that they might enjoy this particular gift in the life of the Church and thus each in one's own way, may be of some advantage to the salvific mission of the Church" (*LG* 43). This leads to the second issue.

This link between consecrated life and the nature and mission of the entire Church is essential to an understanding of the Council's teaching in *PC*. Truly a gift to the whole Church, religious life is more than an opportunity to grow in one's individual spirituality; it is more than living that spirituality in community, as vital as that is. Indeed, religious life is a sign and a gift to all the baptized of the perfection in holiness to which all are called.

Perfectae Caritatis develops this theme further. There are many forms of religious life. Some communities are contemplative, others are active in the world, still others are monastic. Some members are also members of the clergy; most are not. Such a variety of gifts enriches the Church. The decree encourages each religious order to study carefully "the spirit and the aims" of their founders. This is more than a historical exercise; by recovering the vision of their founders, congregations can "attune" that original vision to "the changed conditions of our time."

Perhaps the most significant aspect of Vatican II's treatment of religious life is the fact that the bishops created a strong theological basis for religious life by including it in chapters 5 and 6 of *Lumen Gentium*. Despite the tensions surrounding the preparation of *PC*, the document builds on that foundation by describing religious life in terms of following Christ and building up the body of Christ in the world.

After the Council

The journey of religious life has been as complicated and contentious after the Council as it was before. There were visible signs of internal change within most religious institutes. In many parishes and schools, sisters shifted from their former full-length habits into a much-simplified version. As dramatic as these external changes were, they were nothing compared to the internal shifts going on. Some religious congregations wanted vowed members to remain in long habits and focus on their own interior spirituality. Others welcomed innovative adaptations of living religious life more "in the world," with religious serving as theologians, doctors, attorneys, in diocesan and national leadership, and so on. These tensions showed no sign of abatement. The Vatican instituted an "apostolic visitation" (investigation) into women's religious orders in the United States, but it withered under criticism, especially from laypeople, that sisters' creativity and service were signs of vitality.

One powerful voice on the vitality of religious life since the Council is Sister Sandra Schneiders of the Sisters of the Immaculate Heart of Mary (IHM). A theologian and scripture scholar, Sister Sandra has also written powerfully on religious life itself: "I have little doubt that, consciously or unconsciously, the tension in the contemporary Church which is focused by, but definitely not limited to, the struggle over the Council is what is really at the base of the current investigation of Religious. Getting Religious back in male-mandated dress, officially enclosed houses, institutional apostolates controlled by the clergy, under the control of compliant superiors who see themselves as delegates of the hierarchy are expressions of a deeper agenda, namely, the neutralizing of the prophetic role of Religious in the Church. In our time, that neutralization is in the service of the reversal of the conciliar renewal....But nothing constructive can be built on denial of what is actually going on. We can build a house for Wisdom only on the bedrock of truth." Sister Sandra's powerful comments serve as a reminder of the prophetic role of all believers in general, and of consecrated religious in particular.

THE PRIESTLY ORDERS OF BISHOPS AND PRESBYTERS

As we will discuss in more detail later, there are two ways or modes of participation in the sacrament of holy orders: the priestly (sacerdotal) and the diaconal. Properly speaking, when we use the term "priest" we are referring to both presbyters and bishops. This section will deal with both priestly ministries while the next section will address the ministry of deacons.

During the Council

As we have already seen in the previous section on religious life, the bishops divided the work in two: one Commission dealt with the theological foundations and another dealt with its pastoral applications. Without drawing too sharp a distinction, one could say that the treatment of bishops in chapter 3 ("On the Hierarchical Structure of the Church and in Particular on the Episcopate.") of *Lumen Gentium* (§§18–29) offers a strong theological foundation for the applications developed in subsequent decrees about the episcopate and the presbyterate. (The diaconate does not have its own "application" decree.) The structure of chapter 3 is significant. Paragraphs 18 to 27 deal in various ways with the nature of the episcopate and its relationship to the papacy and to the local Church as well as the Church Universal. Only one paragraph (§28) attends to the presbyterate, and one paragraph (§29) to the diaconate. Clearly, the intent of the bishops was to develop and emphasize the nature of the episcopate, and then to situate the presbyterate and diaconate as the primary assistants and collaborators in the bishop's ministry. As theologian and Cardinal Walter Kasper has explained, the presbyterate and the diaconate are the "two arms" of the bishop.

The bishops had strong disagreements over the subject of episcopal collegiality. In an interview with the author, retired Bishop Gerald O'Keefe shared that most of the bishops supported the notion that bishops are successors of the apostles. However, a strong vocal minority argued against such a position. The final decision of the Council was in favor of apostolic collegiality. It was further explained that ordination as a bishop constituted his membership in the college of bishops. This college of bishops, always in communion with the bishop of Rome at its head, and never apart from him, participates in the universal care of the Church.

Lumen Gentium also addressed another contentious issue—the sacramental nature of episcopal ordination. For centuries, theologians had debated whether consecration as a bishop was a sacrament in itself. Some had held that bishops were "above" the sacrament of holy orders and administered it; others suggested that bishops were, essentially, priests who had been given additional jurisdiction by the pope. *Lumen Gentium* resolved the issue: a bishop's ordination is sacramental, and his power flows from that sacrament. While he must always serve in communion with the pope, the bishop is not the pope's vicar. Through his participation in the sacrament of holy orders, he serves collaboratively with the pope and other bishops in the universal governance of the Church as well as in the governance of the diocese for which he is responsible. The diocese, with the bishop at its head, and surrounded by other ministers and the faithful, is the basic expression of the one, holy, catholic, and apostolic Church (*LG* 26).

After the Council

Christus Dominus (*CD*) reflects these themes in its introduction. They are further developed in the three major chapters of the decree. Interestingly, chapter 1 deals with the responsibility of the bishop in his universal role before turning to his diocesan ministry in chapter 2. Many bishops discussed the desire to continue the kind of collegial approach being taken at the Council; to this end, they would recommend to the Holy Father that a permanent synodal structure be established as part of the Roman Curia. Furthermore, the document encourages the reform of the Roman Curia further to be of better support and service to the individual bishops as well as their episcopal conferences. Pope Francis took significant steps in both these areas.

Chapter 2 of *CD* turns to the ministry of the bishop in his assigned diocese. The bishop's ministry is described as a true *diakonia*, a ministry of service expressed through the functions of word, sacrament, and charity. Those who are ordained or installed into formal ministry in a diocese share in that threefold ministry of the bishop. Chapter 3 further expresses the desire of the bishops to extend the work of consultation, collegiality, and subsidiarity they were experiencing at the Council. It affirms the value of regional episcopal conferences and other such extra-diocesan structures. In a way, one could say that the bishops were trying to replicate their conciliar experience on universal, regional, and diocesan levels.

The ministry and life of presbyters, addressed briefly

in *LG* 28, finds fuller expression in the decree *Presbyterorum Ordinis* (*PO*). In chapter 1, the ministry of the presbyter is described in traditional terms. The priest receives a sacred power to offer the sacrifice, to forgive sins, and so on. But in the context of *LG* 28, all this is seen as part of the identity of the Church as a "priestly people," and the role of the priest is to empower the whole people of God to exercise the priestly character of baptism. He does not live and act in isolation, nor is he called to a higher order of spiritual perfection; recall our earlier discussion on religious life. Rather, the ministry of the priest is to help all people seek spiritual perfection, regardless of their state of life. Chapter 2 grounds this ministry in Christ, Priest, Prophet, and King, describing the priest's ministry of the word, sacrament, and charity. While *PO* reflected a fresh look at the exercise of the ministerial priesthood, it left many things unsaid. In the overall context of the Council's teaching on ministry, the priest now had to see himself as one minister among many: the laity and religious were called to public ministry in the Church and the world, too, and the diaconate was being strengthened, reformed, and was now serving as a permanent order of ordained ministry.

This situation was certainly made more complex by the decree on the formation of priests, *Optatam Totius* (*OT*). It strongly recommended a decentralization of seminary formation and held that each bishop or bishops' conference should set their own curricula and seminary procedures; until then, that had been a responsibility of the Vatican's Congregation for Seminaries and Universities. Now, seminary formation would begin to explore new theological directions, find ways to integrate priestly formation with other forms of education for ministry, and develop practical pastoral skills. Finally, *OT* focused on the spiritual, intellectual, and pastoral growth of the seminarian. These themes would be further developed in 1990 when John Paul II convened an Ordinary Synod on priestly formation. In his post-Synodal Exhortation *Pastores Dabo Vobis* (1992), he described four pillars of priestly formation, adding the human dimension to the spiritual, academic, and pastoral dimensions.

THE SERVANT ORDER OF DEACONS

Unfortunately, it became rather common, shortly after the Council, to begin speaking of two kinds of deacons: "transitional" deacons who were ordained in the seminary while on the way to eventual ordination as presbyters, and "permanent" deacons who remain deacons. While understandable, it shows a poor understanding of the meaning of ordination. Essentially, *all* ordinations are "permanent"—once ordained, always ordained. Any person ordained as a deacon remains a deacon, even if he is later ordained a presbyter or a bishop. Sometimes we will see a bishop wear a deacon's dalmatic under the chasuble of a priest. He does so because he remains a deacon. Imagine a priest who becomes a bishop. We would never refer to that new bishop as a "transitional" priest. Therefore, a deacon is a deacon is a deacon. There is no such thing as a "transitional" deacon and to speak of a "permanent" deacon is redundant.

In the ancient and early medieval Church, deacons emerged as powerful ministers in the life of the Church, usually as the principal assistants to their bishops. They were heavily involved in the life of the Church as overseers of the Church's temporal goods, as legates from their bishops to other bishops and regional authorities, and so on. Frequently, they would be elected to serve as bishop following the death of their predecessors. As the theology of holy orders developed in new directions in the twelfth and thirteenth centuries, the diaconate—already in decline—assumed a largely liturgical and ornamental role, a final step taken before ordination to the presbyterate.

At the Council of Trent in the sixteenth century, there were proposals made to bring back a more substantive diaconate as in the early Church, but these proposals were never implemented. The early nineteenth century saw preliminary suggestions that, because of the scriptural foundations of the diaconate, deacons should again become a feature of the modern Church. These conversations continued, largely in Germany, Italy, and France, well into the twentieth century. But it was in the death camps of the Second World War, especially at Dachau, that the priest-prisoners began to envision the need for deacons in a postwar world. Many of these priests wrote about their wartime discussions after the war, drawing the attention of church officials, laity, and theologians such as Karl Rahner. In the late 1940s and throughout the 1950s, discussions about deacons featured prominently at international conferences on catechesis and liturgy. By the time of the Council, the voices of nearly 200 bishops comprised 101 proposals concerning the possibility of a diaconate exercised permanently; only 11 of those proposals were against the idea, representing just 26 bishops. The idea of a renewed diaconate had captured the imagination of many of the bishops from around the world, while its biggest supporters were from Europe. Bishops from developing nations would later adopt the idea as well.

During the Council

The first draft of *LG* did not contain any reference to the diaconate. However, the bishops were not satisfied with this draft for many reasons, and the diaconate appears in the three subsequent drafts. While the diaconate is mentioned briefly in five conciliar documents, the most significant, as we have seen, is *LG* 29, which consists of two major sections. The first section describes the diaconate in a fifth-century text that says that deacons are ordained "not unto the priesthood, but unto a ministry of service" (*non ad sacerdotium sed ad ministerium*). The precise nature of this unspecified "service" will emerge as being problematic in the ensuing years. That fifth-century text is a modification of the third-century *Apostolic Tradition*: "When the deacon is ordained, this is the reason why the bishop alone shall lay his hands upon him: he is not ordained to the priesthood but to serve the bishop and to carry out the bishop's commands" (*non ad sacerdotium sed in ministerio episcopi*). Such a specific character of "service" as service to the bishop will develop slowly after the Council. What is particularly interesting is that the conciliar debate about the diaconate took place in the middle of the debate on the episcopate. The diaconate was clearly being seen as an extension of the bishop's own ministry, which the bishops had already called a *diakonia*.

Lumen Gentium continues to refer to the sacramental grace associated with the diaconate, confirming the sacramental significance of the deacon's ordination. This was to counter the often-heard expression of a "lay" deacon. In the Catholic Church, such an expression is not possible, since from the earliest days of the Church deacons have been part of the ordained clergy. Unfortunately, one still hears this error, sometimes even in Catholic circles. Deacons serve in communion with the bishops and their priests, and like them, serve in a *diakonia* of word, sacrament, and charity. Finally, the first section of *LG* 29 concludes with a partial list of possible functions for the deacon, namely "to administer baptism solemnly, to be custodian and dispenser of the Eucharist, to assist at and bless marriages in the name of the Church, to bring Viaticum to the dying, to read the Sacred Scripture to the faithful, to instruct and exhort the people, to preside over the worship and prayer of the faithful, to administer sacramentals, to officiate at funeral and burial services." If the bishops had concluded with this section, even the seminary diaconate would have been affirmed and strengthened. But the bishops go further.

In the second section, the bishops talk about the essential need for the ministries of the deacon and that, to make them more available, ordaining older married candidates to a diaconate permanently exercised would be possible in the future. Such a decision was to be reserved for the Holy See after receiving a request from the episcopal conferences. The bishops would later establish the minimum age of thirty-five for the married ordinands. Younger candidates were to remain celibate.

After the Council

Pope Paul VI implemented this decision two years after the Council, and the diaconate quickly developed, especially in many parts of Europe (where the original idea had emerged) and the United States. In 1998, the Congregation for Catholic Education issued "Basic Norms for the Formation of Permanent Deacons," and the Congregation for Clergy issued the "Directory for the Ministry and Life for Permanent Deacons." These two documents further refined the formation, ministry, and life of the diaconate, and in most countries, national directories have been created to implement specific details, giving a greater consistency to the experience of the diaconate. The diaconate initially grew rapidly. For example, in 2003, the Archdiocese of Galveston-Houston ordained ninety-nine deacons in one year (sixty English-speaking deacons and thirty-nine Spanish-speaking deacons), and had to separate the group into three ordination ceremonies to accommodate the numbers. Annual ordination class sizes were not always so large, of course, but many dioceses reported groups of fifteen to twenty or more every year.

An emerging issue, especially in the United States, however, is the aging of the diaconate. The bishops at the Council, as John Paul II was quick to point out, envisioned a younger diaconate, still involved with their secular careers, raising families, and so on. The presence of deacons in the workplace, schools, and in other nontraditional areas would increase the Church's influence in those fields, in addition to service within the Church itself. The latest statistics, however, confirm something that has been developing for years: namely, that most deacons in the United States are well over sixty-five, and almost no deacons are under forty. While international statistics are not available on this issue, anecdotal reporting suggests that this is a universal problem. Currently, ordinations to the diaconate are not keeping pace with deaths and retirements. Unless strategies are pursued to reverse this trend, the future of the renewed diaconate is questionable.

CONCLUSION

The notion of official ministry went through significant development at the Council, all of it based solidly on the Council's emerging ecclesiology. Whether discussing the role of the laity, professed religious, or the ordained ministries—all of it was based on an ecclesiology grounded in baptism and the rights and obligations of every member of the faithful. The reform and renewal of the Church's self-understanding is reflected in the resulting reform and renewal of the ministries of the Church.

The Church is alive, and thus in a constant state of reform and renewal, which means the Church's ministries must do likewise. Whether speaking of consecrated life or the ordained ministries, each of which has its own challenges and potential, the notion of constant change and growth is an essential characteristic. As Cardinal Newman wrote, "To live is to change; to live well is to have changed often."

What needs to be addressed today and in the future?

First, more work needs to be done to develop a contemporary theology of the episcopate. It is an interesting fact that, as central as the Council's concern was for a proper understanding of the episcopacy, very little theological work has been done since the Council on developing that understanding. It is intriguing to realize that, while there are detailed formation processes for those entering religious life, the priesthood, or the diaconate, no true formation is offered to men entering the episcopate.

Second, the Synod of Bishops, established by Paul VI at the request of the world's bishops at the Council, was intended by the bishops as a means of extending the kind of consultation and collaboration they were experiencing in the Council. Unfortunately, these postconciliar synods have been uneven in their application, depending on the intentions and visions of the pope who convened them. Certainly, under Pope Francis we are seeing an approach to synods and synodality that is far more in keeping with the original conciliar intent for synods to be true events of episcopal collegiality and decision-making.

Third, the presbyterate is still struggling to find its own sacramental identity, and there remains a tension between those who retreat into a more cultic understanding of the priesthood and those who look for a broader meaning. In 2021, the study, "Introducing the 2021 Survey of American Catholic Priests: Overview and Selected Findings," by Brad Vermurlen, Stephen Cranney, and Mark Regnerus, reported that 51 percent of priests are "pessimistic about the state of the church." The survey also revealed a deepening rift between younger priests, who are more politically conservative, and their older counterparts. A significant number of priests also expressed concerns over their relationship with their bishops, especially strained over the sex abuse crisis.

Fourth, the question of whether women might be ordained to the diaconate remains a topic of interest at every level of the Church. This includes two consecutive iterations of the International Theological Commission under the direction of then Cardinal Joseph Ratzinger, during the papacy of John Paul II, and more recently two pontifical commissions convened by Pope Francis.

We end where we began, by observing that we are still *in medias res*, still in the middle of things. The great Church historian Hubert Jedin observed that it takes about a century to implement the decisions of a general Council such as Vatican II. We have a long way to go. It might be tempting to look at the challenges outlined here and lose heart. Instead, these challenges can be seen as a sign of hope. Most religious are finding new ways to serve and challenge us all to be better than we are. Most of our bishops are honest, hardworking pastors who seek only to serve the people of God entrusted to them. Most of our presbyters, likewise, are doing wonderful work in the vineyard despite unbelievable pressures. And deacons have found the need for their service across the whole spectrum of society in addition to their parishes.

FOR FURTHER READING

Confoy, Maryanne. *Religious Life and Priesthood: Perfectae Caritatis, Optatam Totius, and Presbyterorum Ordinis*. Mahwah, NJ: Paulist Press, 2008.

Ditewig, William T. *Courageous Humility: Reflections on the Church, Diakonia, and Deacons*. Mahwah, NJ: Paulist Press, 2022.

———. *The Emerging Diaconate: Servant Leaders in a Servant Church*. Mahwah, NJ: Paulist Press, 2007.

Osborne, Kenan. *Priesthood: A History of Ordained Ministry in the Roman Catholic Church*. Eugene, OR: Wipf and Stock, 2003.

Schneiders, Sandra M. *Buying the Field: Catholic Religious Life in Mission to the World*. Mahwah, NJ: Paulist Press, 2013.

———. *Prophets in Their Own Country: Women Religious Bearing Witness to the Gospel in a Troubled Church*. Maryknoll, NY: Orbis Books, 2011.

Witherup, Ronald D., et al. *Ministerial Priesthood in the Third Millennium: Faithfulness of Christ, Faithfulness of Priests*. Collegeville, MN: Liturgical Press, 2009.

5

ECUMENISM AND INTERRELIGIOUS DIALOGUE

Stephanie M. Wong

The three Vatican II documents that address religious and ecclesial diversity—the declaration *Nostra Aetate* (1965), and the decrees *Unitatis Redintegratio* (1964) and *Orientalium Ecclesiarum* (1964)—continue to inspire Catholics toward respectful engagement with the religious other, while also creating new puzzles of contextualizing faith within global Catholicism. In this chapter, we will survey these three documents, note several controversies in their interpretation since 2000, and point to two unfolding developments in the twenty-first century: grappling with the sociological reality of migration and engaging an ecclesial reconception of the Church concerned with human welfare. These Vatican II documents aspired to a new mode of respectful engagement and dialogue, intending to distance the Church from past patterns of triumphalism toward non-Christians, competition with Protestants, and paternalism toward the Eastern Catholic Churches. This was a major change in attitude and approach.

A SUMMARY OF THE DOCUMENTS

Nostra Aetate

No doubt, the most well-known of the documents on religious diversity is *Nostra Aetate* (Declaration on the Relation of the Church to Non-Christian Religions), promulgated on October 28, 1965. This statement arose out of a concern to address the relationship of the Church to the Jewish people in the wake of the Holocaust, though it was broadened to address non-Christian communities in general.

Nostra Aetate begins in panoramic scope, characterizing all peoples as participating in a shared human condition with a shared capacity to perceive "that hidden power which hovers over the course of things and over the events of human history" (§2). After affirming the sincerity of other religious inquiries—for instance, in the Hindu philosophical investigation of divine mystery, and the Buddhist recognition of this world's changeability—the declaration then issues its most oft-quoted line: "The Catholic Church rejects nothing that is true and holy in these religions. She regards with sincere reverence those ways of conduct and of life, those precepts and teachings which, though differing in many aspects from the ones she holds and sets forth, nonetheless often reflect a ray of that Truth which enlightens all men" (§2). This affirmed a crucial conceptual space between "the Catholic Church" and "the Truth," allowing that the Catholic Church might see truth and yet not be the only religious community to do so.

The remainder of *Nostra Aetate* focuses upon the Abrahamic traditions of Islam and Judaism: the Church "regards with esteem" the Muslims for their efforts to submit wholeheartedly to God, while noting disagreement over Jesus's divinity (§3). The Church also affirms Christianity's indebtedness to the Jews, the people to whom God first issued revelation. In fact, *NA* affirms that "God holds the Jews most dear for the sake of their Fathers; he does not repent of the gifts He makes or of the calls He issues"—a statement that counteracts any simplistic supersessionist account of Christians replacing the Jews in the eyes of God. On the contrary, *NA* hopes for a time in which peoples might together face God and, quoting Zephaniah 3:9, "serve him shoulder to shoulder" (§4). Throughout, the document urges Christians to put away the interreligious hostilities of the past and treat people of other religions with respect.

Unitatis Redintegratio

Unitatis Redintegratio (Decree on Ecumenism) came earlier in the historical unfolding of the Council, promulgated along with *Orientalium Ecclesiarum* (Decree on the Catholic Churches of the Eastern Rite) in November 1964. They were less controversial than *Nostra Aetate* but contained important affirmations on ecclesial diversity.

Unitatis Redintegratio opens with a statement of desire for the restoration of unity among Christians. It stresses the regrettable state of division in the body of Christ but abstains from blaming non-Catholic Christians for it. Rather than casting Orthodox and Protestant Christians as heretical or schismatic, as had been done for centuries, *UR* simply speaks of "separated brethren" who also desire Christian unity under the grace of the Holy Spirit. Just as in *Nostra Aetate*, the denominationalism of the Roman Catholic Church as such is not ultimate. Throughout, *UR* speaks more transcendently of "the Church of God" and "the Church of Christ."

The subsequent chapters then provide to Catholics some principles of ecumenism that offer a Christocentric and Spiritcentric vision of the Church. Christ is "the principle of the Church's unity" and the Holy Spirit "has not refrained from using them as means of salvation which derive their efficacy from the very fullness of grace and truth entrusted to the Church" (§3). So, although the document does regard separated Church communities as "deficient in some respects" or "in disagreement," this should not be taken as a totalizing or final judgment. *Unitatis Redintegratio* endorses the ecumenical movement and urges Catholics to participate in dialogue with other Christians.

In discussing the Eastern Churches that are not in communion with Rome—for instance, the Eastern Orthodox Churches, Oriental Orthodox Churches, the Assyrian Church of the East—the decree affirms the sincerity of their faith, their heritage in the traditions of the apostles, their insight into the mystery of revelation, and the validity of their apostolic succession and sacraments. Turning then to the Western Churches not in communion with Rome (i.e., Protestant or Independent communities) the decree is more reserved, worrying especially about differences in the interpretation of revealed truth. *Unitatis Redintegratio* affirms these Christians' devotion to Scripture and the efficacy of rebirth in baptism as instituted by Christ, generally characterizing their faith as a genuine witness to Christ.

Orientalium Ecclesiarum

Finally, the decree *Orientalium Ecclesiarum* affirms the diversity of those Catholic Churches in the East that have different rites. Though an oversimplification, there are basically three families of historic churches. From the ancient center of Alexandria come the Coptic Catholic and Ethiopian Catholic Churches. From Antioch come the Byzantine Catholic, Armenian Catholic, Maronite Catholic, Malankara Catholic,

West Syrian Catholic, Chaldean Catholic, and Malabar Catholic Churches. From Rome come the Ambrosian and Mozarabic Churches, and, most familiar to Catholics in the Americas, the Roman Catholic Church. The decree acknowledges their ancient apostolicity and affirms their equal dignity (§3). The main call of the decree was to recognize the right of these Eastern Catholic Churches to keep distinct liturgical practices, rather than becoming Latinized. This concern arises out of a context of several centuries of mission efforts from Western colonial powers whose conversionary efforts and presence led to a Latinization of practice in places like South India. The exhortation was framed therefore in terms of retrieval: to "take steps to return to their ancestral traditions" (§6), with the hope for these churches to embrace a heritage both ancient and organic.

The decree goes on to affirm that the Eastern Rite Churches can and must have autonomous powers. For instance, the patriarchs or major archbishops are, with their synod, the highest authority for any business within the territory of the patriarchate. This involves the right to appoint bishops (§9), set the liturgical calendar with dates like Easter (§22), and regulate the usage of languages in sacred worship (§23). At the same time, *OE* maintains the primacy of the Roman pontiff who has the "inalienable right...to intervene in individual cases" (§9). The decree thus performs a move that is slightly ironic insofar as it affirms local autonomy practice, while being itself a Rome-issued document. This has created complications globally in cases where the local community disagrees about which chapter of historical practice is most essential to their local identity.

Orientalium Ecclesiarum also has a section on the "separated" Eastern Churches that attempts to modulate relations between the Eastern Catholic and Eastern Orthodox Churches, introducing an ecumenical thrust that pulls in some tension with the rest of the text. The decree charges the Eastern Rite Churches with a "special duty of promoting the unity of all Christians, especially Eastern Christians" (§24). Practically, the decree reiterates the Catholic permission for Eastern Orthodox believers to receive sacraments of penance, Eucharist, and anointing of the sick; and it allows for Catholics to partake in these sacraments from Orthodox ministers when unable to access a Catholic priest (§25). The document supports communion in worship (*communicatio in sacris*) for pastoral purposes, so long as it does not bring scandal or indifferentism. On the one hand, this ecumenical gesture seems logical given the Decree on Ecumenism and its call for warmer ecumenical relations. Yet, on the other hand, this brings *OE* to conclude along a different vector than the rest of the text. For, although *OE* opens with affirmations of the internal diversity among the Catholic Churches, it ends with a potentially more homogenizing picture of ecclesial unity. As discussed below, the Eastern Churches have hotly debated whether *OE* resolves or exacerbates the challenges of trying to realize unity in diversity.

TWENTY-FIRST-CENTURY DEVELOPMENTS

Nostra Aetate

Conversations in post–Vatican II theology of religions have explored how the life of the Church may participate in but not exhaust the truth or mystery of God, recognizing the value of the religious insights of others. In the decades since its promulgation, *Nostra Aetate* has fostered robust debates in theology of religions and world Christianity. In subsequent Roman statements such as Paul VI's apostolic exhortation *Evangelii Nuntiandi* (1975), John Paul II's encyclical *Redemptoris Missio* (1990), and the Pontifical Council for Interreligious

Dialogue's "Dialogue and Proclamation" (1991), the Catholic magisterium has generally promoted an "inclusivist" interpretation of *Nostra Aetate* that tries both to affirm the necessity of Christ for salvation and to acknowledge that Christians can learn from engaging in dialogue with others. But this raises further questions about whether it is a narrow or wide inclusivism: Are these other rays of truth ones that Christianity already makes explicit, and therefore not to be regarded as adding anything new? Are they rays that Christianity already holds implicitly, but are brought to explicit light through the beneficial lens of other wisdom traditions? Or does Christianity fail to register some truths at all, since different religions have eyes to see substantively different rays?

The most fervent academic debates over the theology of religions unfolded at the turn of the millennium, with sometimes fractious relations between the Holy See and scholars who grappled with religious plurality and called for some theological embrace of it. In the early 2000s, what was then the Congregation of the Doctrine of the Faith investigated North American theologians such as Jacques Dupuis, Peter Phan, and Elizabeth Johnson for theological exploration and propositions in this area. Since 2010, a newer subfield known as "comparative theology" has taken up the question of interreligious reflection in what is perhaps both a methodologically more humble and politically safer mode. Catholic comparative theologians like Francis Clooney often explicitly bracket questions about the saving character of other religions, encouraging scholars and practitioners simply to listen attentively to what their sacred texts, interpretive traditions, and ritual practices might have to say. In this bracketing, comparative theologians hope to avoid imposing a Christian preoccupation with salvation upon other religious traditions that may care about other religious questions. This approach also holds at bay the freighted issue of whether the Church has a privileged vantage on truth.

Meanwhile, the global Church has undertaken the work of interreligious dialogue in context-specific ways, often as a matter of cultural inculturation, economic justice, and peace-building. For instance, the Federation of Asian Bishops' Conferences (FABC) and its consulting theologians stress the integral character of dialoguing with both the religions and the poor of Asia, insisting that both are necessary for the Church to become "of" Asia rather than a foreign missionary presence. Meanwhile, African leaders like Cardinal Francis Arinze of Nigeria have promoted dialogue to find common ground with Muslims, primarily with the goal of forestalling religious misunderstanding and violence in West Africa. Around the world, Catholic communities have taken to heart the task of inculturation as an incarnational process of the "Word" of faith taking on the "flesh" of the religio-social locality.

Voices from the global Church, however, have also warned against forgetting the Jewish character of Jesus. For instance, such diverse thinkers as the Gambian Catholic Lamin Sanneh and the Austrian-born Catholic Judith Gruber have pointed out that the incarnation paradigm may too often assume and reinscribe a Greek or generically Western conception of the Christian faith as that which must be incarnated into the religio-cultural margins. In that sense, it is useful to keep in mind *Nostra Aetate*'s original attention to the genesis of early Christian communities amid the Second Temple Judaism of Roman-ruled Palestine. It is also necessary to recall the original context for the drafting of the document in the wake of the Shoah. At the Council, promoters of the decree were conscious that Catholics have too often forgotten the distinct religio-cultural heritage of Jesus, and so they invited the Church to reckon with its production of supersessionist theologies and

Catholics' all too frequent participation in antisemitic rhetoric and violence.

Unitatis Redintegratio

Unitatis Redintegratio was easily passed in Vatican II's conciliar votes and generally well-received by Protestants glad for its nonhostile and non-zero-sum approach to ecclesial diversity. Subsequent decades saw lively efforts at ecumenical dialogue that reached into the twentieth century. For instance, the Joint International Commission for Theological Dialogue between the Catholic Church and Orthodox Church has met every two to four years from 1980 to 2016. So too, the Catholic-Lutheran dialogue reached a milestone in 1999 when Lutherans and Catholics signed a "common declaration" on justification, a key topic of theological contention in the sixteenth-century Reformation.

But overall, the ecumenical movement's early energy has cooled in the opening decades of the twenty-first century. This is not so much because the parties involved no longer believe in the good of ecumenical relations or the hope of Christian unity, but more because they face pressing concerns within. In the East, Orthodoxy has seen heated disagreements that arise from the national organization of many Orthodox Churches. For example, in May 2022, the Ukrainian Orthodox Church, amid political tensions over Russia's expansion into the Crimean Peninsula, formally cut ties and declared independence from the Russian Orthodox Church and its patriarchate in Moscow. In the West, the traditional mainline Protestant churches have seen a massive drop in church attendance in both Western Europe and North America and so have been increasingly worried about survival within their particular cultures of secularity and materialism.

Moreover, *Unitatis Redintegratio* is silent on newer Christian-identifying religious movements that may be non-trinitarian or hold an entirely different formula and understanding of baptism and its role in salvation. For instance, the decree makes no mention of groups like the Jehovah's Witnesses, Christian Scientists, Church of Latter-Day Saints, Oneness Pentecostals, Unification Church (Moonies), Shincheonji Church of Jesus, various African-initiated churches that are non-trinitarian belief or baptism, or the Jesus-affirming adherents of the Insider Movement within Islam. As the historic Protestant churches of European origin shrink and these other communities gain strength globally, the silence of *UR* on these communities becomes even more notable. Since the document mainly addresses those Protestants for whom a trinitarian baptism could be affirmed as a shared "beginning" for fuller unity (§22), it remains uncontroversial but also increasingly irrelevant to the more lively debates about who claims to be and is recognized as a follower of Christ.

Orientalium Ecclesiarum

As noted earlier, the stakes of *Orientalium Ecclesiarum* in the twentieth and twenty-first centuries have varied widely but mattered deeply to those communities for whom the call to return to their ancestral tradition meant distilling what their contextual needs or traditional practices might be. Initially, some were disappointed that *OE* did not go further in promoting a more robust ecumenism between the Eastern Catholic and Eastern Orthodox Churches. For instance, the Melkite Greek Catholic Archbishop Elias Zoghby had hoped that Vatican II might open and chart a way toward double communion. He hailed originally from Egypt so was concerned about the rift between the Melkite Catholic and Antiochian Orthodox

Churches there. From his vantage, *OE* fell short by only tepidly recommending that members of the Eastern Catholic and Eastern Orthodox Churches partake in each other's sacraments in times of exigency. Granted, the Orthodox had not even agreed to these provisions. Nonetheless, for Zoghby and other Eastern Catholics primarily concerned with relations with the Orthodox, the decree did not go nearly far enough on the Catholic side in trying to open possibilities for intercommunion or in realizing a warmer, boundary-transcending, ecumenical unity.

In the past two decades, what has most racked the global Catholic Church are divisions within some Eastern Churches over how to carry out their liturgical rites vis-à-vis Latin-Rite Catholicism. To understand this, two issues must be kept in mind. First, there is the historical fact that Western exploration, colonialism, and missionary work expanded the Latin-Rite Catholic Church around the globe. This means the cultural and liturgical Latinization of the Eastern communities had already been underway, in some cases, for hundreds of years. Second, there is the organizational reality that various Eastern and Latin communities often exist, not only as distinct liturgical "rites," but each as *sui juris* church with different jurisdictions in the same geographical region.

Take, for instance, the Catholic churches of India where Syro-Malabar, Syro-Malankara, and Latin Catholics all exist today. The Syro-Malabar and Syro-Malankara communities are older, tracing their origins back to the missionary efforts of the apostle St. Thomas in southern India. However, Portuguese power in the sixteenth century established Latin communities and then forcibly incorporated former Syrian-Rite communities into the Latin-Rite structures. Although the Holy See did begin restoring a native hierarchy in 1923, only those regions most dense with Syro-Malabar or Syro-Malankara communities were restored and granted non-Latin ecclesial identity. For this reason, some Syro-Malabar and Syro-Malankara leaders want the continuing Latin-Rite Indian communities returned to their jurisdiction, feeling that any discussion from Rome about the de-Latinization of their liturgies is ironic so long as Latins still hold jurisdictional control over much of the Church in India.

In this context, Vatican II and the promulgation of *Ecclesiarum Orientalium* sparked enormous debate within the Syro-Malabar Catholic community. For if the *sui juris* Syro-Malabar Church was encouraged by Vatican II to return to its "ancestral tradition," then which form of the Eucharistic liturgy or Holy Qurbana should be restored? This controversy has unfolded as both a geographic and ecclesiological disagreement, especially in the state of Kerala. On the one hand, the Archdiocese of Ernakulam changed the celebrant to face the people, and even promoted a revised liturgy for the Latin-Rite, Syro-Malabar, and Syro-Malankara Catholic Churches in India (generally more accepted by those in northern Kerala)—which was then opposed by both the Congregation of Oriental Churches in Rome and the Archdiocese of Changanacherry (southern Kerala). There, on the other hand, some felt that a truly Indian liturgy would honor the Chaldean Syrian Church's long legacy, and even advocated a restoration of the pre-sixteenth-century East Syrian Holy Qurbana. In the south of Kerala, most of the faithful have defended the practice of the celebrant facing the altar.

In 1999, a Synod of Bishops of the Syro-Malabar Church attempted to come to an agreement to unify the celebration of the liturgy. They decreed a compromise that Rome directed to be implemented by 2022: during the Liturgy of the Word, the priest would face the people, and then during the Liturgy of the Eucharist, he would face with the people toward the altar. But several eparchies have resisted this hybrid "Synodal Form," leading to even greater controversy involving hunger strikes, burning of pastoral letters, and even a brawl in the sanctuary of the Ernakulam cathedral basilica in late 2022 that damaged the altar and sacred vessels. All this demonstrates the complexity of trying to implement *OE*'s call for the Eastern Churches to recover their venerable antiquity and distinct traditions, when this is precisely what is contested amid the multiple layers of history and multiple strains of local identities bound up in practice.

THE FUTURE

As we consider the future of these conciliar documents on religious and ecclesial diversity, it is worth noting two developments—one sociological, and one more ecclesial—that will no doubt shape the thinking and practice of Catholicism going forward.

First, the twenty-first century Church grapples with the reality of migration, where the movements of peoples engender more dynamic and complex social situations than the Council initially imagined. Globalization, experienced as a compression of time and space, has put people in closer or more frequent contact with religious others. This is evident in both voluntary migration (of religious pilgrims or transnational workers moving for economic opportunity) and involuntary migration (of those forced to be religious, political, economic, or ecological refugees). These dynamics are then supercharged by the interconnectedness of media, wherein mobile people now easily remain or become aware of what is going on with human communities elsewhere.

For example, the Syro-Malabar controversy has not remained limited to India but exists also in diasporic communities in the United States. Keralan immigrants to the United States find themselves in mixed Syro-Malabar communities, and are highly aware of the tensions between the so-called Latinizers and Chaldeanizers back in India thanks to social media. The question of jurisdiction cannot be treated as either a matter of simple graphic location or as a question of immediate cultural majority since immigrant diasporic communities are often hybrid in both senses. No doubt, the Syro-Malabar bishops today spend fewer minutes debating the date of Easter, one of the issues named in *Ecclesiarum Orientalium*, and far more worrying about the effects of media coverage and social media narratives both in India and the Indian diasporic Catholic communities, where tensions can become inflamed very quickly.

Second, there is an ongoing reconception of the Church itself in the twenty-first century. In the summer of 2022, Pope Francis shocked and intrigued many by reorganizing the Roman Curia. This shook up the traditional relations between conversations about theology, identity in interreligious relations, and spiritual and material welfare. Before, the post–Vatican II Curia structurally privileged "secretariats" and "congregations" (like the heavyweight Congregation for the Doctrine of the Faith) over the "pontifical councils," "commissions," and other offices (like the pontifical councils for Interreligious Dialogue, Justice and Peace, or Pastoral Care of Migrants). However, the new structure of sixteen "dicasteries" puts such issues on more equal footing. For instance, the dicasteries for Evangelization and for the Doctrine of the Faith now sit alongside the Dicastery for Interreligious Dialogue, Dicastery for Promoting Christian Unity, Dicastery for the Eastern Churches, and Dicastery for Promoting Integral Human Development. This restructuring may at first seem like pedantic wordsmithing, but it reflects ongoing debates about the Church's witness in a world of difference.

Indeed, a frank look around seems to affirm that questions of belief and morality must be worked out nowhere other than in the often murky and politically fraught world of human social relations. The COVID-19 pandemic highlighted how the Church's voice and work are always bound up in issues of human concern, but in highly context-specific ways where interdisciplinary reflection is necessary. In mainland China, Catholics at Shijiahui were blamed for meeting for Mass in the initial days of the pandemic. Catholicism was painted there as a public health risk compared to more "responsible" religious and secular groups. Yet in Korea, Catholic bishops were at the forefront of calls to deal with the pandemic in biologically and economically careful ways, while it was the independent Shincheonji Church of Jesus in Daegu, often regarded as a cult by Korean Catholics and mainline Protestants, who caught the media spotlight as an early epicenter of infection.

Meanwhile, nobody knew how to guard against infection in difficult refugee situations of displaced or stateless peoples. For instance, Muslim Rohingya refugees in places like Cox's Bazar, Bangladesh, faced even greater vulnerability amid not only the COVID-19 lockdowns but also horrific fires and floods that hit the camps. In crises like these, even committed interreligious work seems to fall far short of giving people the aid they need for a dignified life. From a Catholic perspective, did the COVID-19 pandemic present a theological, ecumenical, interreligious, or economic problem? Surely, it was all of them, and it is helpful for the Church that the various Roman Dicasteries are structurally encouraged to see such interdisciplinary complexities on a shared plane.

Going forward, it seems the Church will have to grapple increasingly with the implications of migration for interreligious and ecumenical relations. The movement of peoples is no longer an anomalous or fringe phenomenon, but rather the norm. Perhaps the reorganization of the Roman Curia, and the placement of doctrinal issues amid the social interreligious and economic ones, is already a step toward facing that ecclesial reality.

CONCLUSION

In sum, the Vatican II documents on interreligious and ecclesial diversity remain inspiring to many, holding forth the hope of a Catholic Church that can appreciate and honor degrees of variety outside and within. These documents put forth positive affirmations about the sincerity and value of different religious expressions. At the very least, this refreshing change of attitude precludes the Catholic Church from writing off the "religious other" as an object of derision. In many places, *NA*, *UR*, and *OE* demand that Catholics look to see the goodness in their and others' religions with the hope of possibly greater agreement. That said, these Vatican II documents belie the Council's rather static vision of religious cultures. In the 1960s, the Council still conceived a world where people mostly stayed in place and their distinctive traditions of Christianity in the periphery could easily be identified and attributed to them. After the past sixty years of implementing the Council's pro-indigenization, pro-dialogue, and pro-autonomy messages, it is clear that the interreligious and inter-ecclesial affairs of the global Church are more culturally hybrid and historically layered than they ever could have imagined.

FOR FURTHER READING

Clifford, Catherine E., and Massimo Faggioli, eds. *The Oxford Handbook of Vatican II* (part 4, "Reception by Other Christians and Non-Christians"; and part 5, "Global Reception"). Oxford: Oxford University Press, 2023.

Cruz, Gemma Tulud. *Toward a Theology of Migration: Social Justice and Religions Experience.* New York: Palgrave Macmillan, 2014.

Cunningham, Philip A. *Seeking Shalom: The Journey to Right Relationship between Catholics and Jews.* Grand Rapids: Eerdmans, 2015.

Farrugia, Edward. "Re-reading *Orientalium Ecclesiarum.*" *Gregorianum* 88, no. 2 (2007): 352–72.

Fitzgerald, Michael, and John Borelli. *Interfaith Dialogue: A Catholic View.* Maryknoll, NY: Orbis Books, 2006.

Heft, James. *Catholicism and Interreligious Dialogue.* New York: Oxford University Press, 2011.

Joseph, Jaisy. "Of Equal Dignity: An Interpretation of *Orientalium Ecclesiarum.*" *Asian Horizons* 8 no. 1 (2014): 35–47.

Lai, Whalen, and Michael von Brück. *Christianity and Buddhism: A Multicultural History of Their Dialogue.* Maryknoll, NY: Orbis, 2001.

Phan, Peter C., ed. *Christian Theology in the Age of Migration: Implications for World Christianity.* Lanham, MD: Roman & Littlefield, 2020.

Valkenberg, Pim, ed. *A Companion to Comparative Theology.* Leiden: Brill, 2022.

6

EVANGELIZATION AND RELIGIOUS FREEDOM

Miguel H. Díaz

"Error has no rights." The Roman Catholic Church held this position until *Dignitatis Humanae* (*DH*), the Second Vatican Council's Declaration on Religious Freedom. This declaration led to a tectonic shift in Roman Catholic teaching on religious freedom. Signed by Paul VI on December 7, 1965, *DH* was the final document promulgated by the Second Vatican Council. Its teaching on religious freedom changed how the Roman Catholic Church responded to religious perspectives held by Christian churches, religious communities, and persons of no religious affiliation. The inherent dignity of every human person provided the cornerstone of this declaration's groundbreaking affirmation that only people—not ideas—have rights. This new perspective on religious freedom was largely prompted by the need for the Church to adjust to changing worldly and democratic realities. The Church argued that this new teaching could be justified by appealing to both reason and revelation. The trailblazer who prepared this doctrinal evolution was the Jesuit theologian John Courtney Murray.

Murray hailed from the United States, a country that had a long history of defending religious freedom and the separation of church and state. Often characterized as America's first freedom, religious freedom is enshrined in the First Amendment to the U.S. Constitution. It is also a right that many other nations and churches have defended based on human dignity. For instance, the Preamble of the 1948 United Nations Universal Declaration of Human Rights had already recognized fundamental human rights as one of those rights linked to "the recognition of the inherent dignity and of the equal and inalienable rights of all members of the human family." From the perspective of Christian churches, *DH* was also not the first document from a Christian community to affirm religious freedom. In 1948, the First Assembly of the World Council of Churches adopted a "Declaration on Religious Liberty." As Murray observed in a commentary on *DH* the year after Vatican II concluded, "It can hardly be maintained that the Declaration is a milestone in human history—moral, political, or intellectual," adding, "In all honesty it must be admitted that the Church is late in acknowledging the validity of the principle." After the 1948 U.N. declaration, other international covenants and agreements have affirmed this right, including the International Covenant on Civil and Political Rights (1966), the Helsinki Accords (1975), the U.N. Declaration on the Elimination of All Forms of Intolerance and of Discrimination Based on Religion or Belief (1981), and the International Religious Freedom Act (1998).

This chapter will present a summary of the groundbreaking arguments that *DH* proposes with respect to the Church's teaching on religious freedom, which intersects with the Church's obligation to evangelize. Evangelization was discussed in Vatican II's document on missionary activity, *Ad*

Gentes, also promulgated in 1965. We will then explore the reception and unresolved questions related to religious freedom, especially as this fundamental human right has come into tension with other human rights. Finally, the chapter concludes with some brief reflections regarding the future of the teaching of religious freedom, given the missionary nature of the Church and the Christian vocation to evangelize and be living witnesses of the gospel.

DIGNITATIS HUMANAE

The Council's Declaration on Religious Freedom (*DH*) is a short document, modest in scope, and produced after five drafts, two public debates, numerous speeches, interventions, and editorial revisions. While Pope John XXIII's *Pacem in Terris* (*PT*, 1963) had already advocated the right to worship God in accordance with the dictates of conscience, as well as the right to practice religions both privately and publicly (*PT* 14), *DH*'s treatment of religious freedom within the juridical-social order is unprecedented in Roman Catholicism.

Until *DH*, the Roman Catholic Church held claim to what is known as the thesis/hypothesis approach to religious truth and error. The Church maintained that Catholicism alone was the true religion (thesis) and therefore, the only religion deserving legal recognition by any given political establishment. Other religious perspectives could be tolerated as transitional (hypothesis). Looking back at Pius IX's *Syllabus of Errors* (1864) and its rejection of the separation of church and state (so central in the U.S. Constitution), we can appreciate the significant development that *DH* brings regarding religious freedom. True religion, *DH* argues, "subsists" in the Church. The Church, however, is not the sole possessor of truth. All persons are bound to seek truth and, consistent with this claim, *DH* unequivocally declares that all persons are endowed with dignity, are immune from any coercion, and cannot be forced privately or publicly as individuals or as part of a group, to act in a manner contrary to their conscience (*DH* 2).

Upholding the fundamental dignity of every human person, *DH* embraces freedom from coercion. It argues, on the one hand, against forcing anyone to act contrary to their conscience, and on the other hand, against restraining them from acting in accordance with their conscience. All persons retain the right to seek truth in matters concerning religion and in accordance with their dignity and social nature. All are called to cultivate an informed conscience that seeks after truth in what the declaration calls "under use of all suitable means" (*DH* 3). While *DH* does not specify what these suitable means might entail, it sets a solid foundation that moved the Church away from a place of rigidity and absolute truth-claims toward an opened and revolving door that favors ongoing reasoned conversations with worldly realities, including the wisdom that emerges from the world of politics, science, and the humanities. Succinctly summarizing *DH*'s teaching, the Italian sociologist Cardinal Pietro Pavan outlined:

1. Every human person has the right to religious freedom.
2. This right has as its object or content an immunity from coercion at the hands of individuals, social groups, or public powers.
3. The immunity is understood in two senses: (a) no one must be forced to act against his conscience in religious matters; (b) no one must be restrained—in those same religious matters—from acting in conformity with his conscience whether privately or publicly, whether alone or in association with others, within due limits.

4. This right has its foundation in the dignity of the human person as this dignity can be known in the light of revelation as well as through reason.
5. This right demands recognition and sanction in constitutional law whereby society is governed.

RECEPTION AND UNRESOLVED TENSIONS

There is little doubt that *DH* opened the door for Roman Catholic political advocacy on behalf of worldwide religious freedom and evangelization. According to the U.S. Department of State, 74 percent of the world's population lives in countries with serious religious restrictions. Protecting this fundamental right is not only of religious importance for the Roman Catholics, but also for religious minority communities that often face religious prejudice and persecution. Defending this right is not only valuable to religious communities, but it has been shown to be essential in defending the building blocks that structure democratic societies. Signaling the importance of defending religion, the U.S. Department of State maintains an Office of Religious Freedom and an ambassador-at-large. In compliance with the International Religious Freedom Act of 1998, the office publishes annual reports on the state of religious freedom worldwide, challenging violations and working with religious and civic leaders to protect and advance religious freedom and the ability of people to live and share their faith traditions.

Since the Council, the Vatican has remained a strong advocate of religious freedom, actively participating in international conversations and organizations like the United Nations that promote religious freedom. The Vatican and the pope's ambassadors (papal nuncios) have worked closely through diplomatic channels to make sure this fundamental human right is upheld throughout the world. Pope John Paul II, Pope Benedict XVI, and Pope Francis all made significant pronouncements on religious freedom. Pope John Paul II, who was bishop of Krakow during the Council, intervened several times during the process of producing *DH*, often underscoring Christian revelation as foundational for the Church's teaching on religious freedom. As the pope from Poland, a country that was once part of the Soviet Union (1952–89), one could understand why he underscored the need to associate religious freedom and truth. Among other human rights, religious freedom is often undermined and/or suppressed altogether under dictatorial regimes. Pope Benedict XVI echoed his predecessor's approach and focused also on the relationship between religious freedom and the pursuit of world peace. Pope Francis has taken a more diplomatic approach, underscoring the importance of religion to affirm human dignity and as a builder of bridges among peoples.

Notwithstanding these valuable contributions that the Church and its representatives have made since *DH*, religious freedom remains an unfinished project both within and outside the Church. Debates and controversies surrounding its exercise within the United States can be tapped as an example of the questions that *DH* left unaddressed. In 2012, the U.S. Conference of Catholic Bishops' Ad Hoc Committee for Religious Liberty issued a statement titled "Our First, Most Cherished Liberty." In it, the bishops expressed grave concerns about increasing attacks against religious liberty at home and abroad. Although the bishops framed the statement within the global threat to religious freedom, the statement was really drawn in response to the Affordable Care Act (2010) that included coverage in the areas of contraception and women's reproductive rights. The bishops called for the first Fortnight for Freedom to pray and educate Catholics on what they believed were threats to religious freedom.

In defending religious freedom, the U.S. bishops have underscored the argument that "there is no freedom, without the truth." The central challenge is that, since the Council, many Catholics, such as Murray, have abandoned ahistorical, rigid, and essentialist understandings of truth. While Murray underscored how traditional issues relating to natural law needed to be rethought within concrete, existential, and experiential categories, the bishops have continued to insist on a particular understanding of the natural law tradition underscoring the need for Catholics to abide by the "truths about human nature." In this sense, unlike their episcopal predecessors during the 1960s who championed Murray's teaching on religious freedom and its historical consciousness (inspired by the American democratic project and the Establishment Clause), many U.S. bishops today fail to recognize fully how the democratic ideals of inclusion, participation, and historical consciousness not only fueled the very development of the Church's teaching on religious freedom, but also continue to foster new thinking and doctrinal development within the Church. This is particularly relevant to new questions that have emerged related to familial relationships, gender, and sexuality. These are questions that often tap into the dignity of marginalized communities, their religious views and theologies, and their perspectives on life.

In recent times, Roman Catholic Church leaders have been caught in legal battles that surround the exercise of religious freedom. Their legal arguments have been taken all the way to the Supreme Court. These legal battles over religious freedom in the public square, such as cases where Roman Catholic teachers have been fired based on same-sex relations (and legally justified because of the Church's appeal to the ministerial exception), signal two underdeveloped and unresolved areas in *DH*. The first is the question of Christian freedom within the Church, and the second is the question of when governments can legitimately limit the exercise of religious freedom, which could include the freedom and ability to evangelize.

Murray rightly observes that *DH* does not undertake to explore a theology of freedom in line with the evolution of Roman Catholic theological perspectives that, as he put it, "view issues of natural law within the concrete context of the present historic-existential order of grace." In other words, a richer treatment of this fundamental human right invites the theological incorporation of ideas that would require the Church as an institution to embrace *ad intra* the plurality of theological perspectives and distinct opinions of religiously informed consciences with respect to difficult and controversial human experiences and practices, as is often the case in areas related to sexuality and sexual reproduction. Regarding the question of government interference, *DH* recognizes that religious ideas can be weaponized against persons and communities, and that under these circumstances governments have a right to intervene to prevent undermining public order (*DH* 7). But *DH* fails to delineate any guidance on what might justify such interference. As the history of left-wing and right-wing dictatorships demonstrates, one often finds the appeal to public order deployed as a means to silence religion and the voices of religious minorities.

Dignitatis Humanae is the only document from the Second Vatican Council that is addressed to the world. As such, the declaration was primarily concerned with discussing where the Church stood with respect to acknowledging religious freedom as a human and civic right. To be sure, the declaration does make the theological claim that Christian revelation, faith, and doctrine ultimately ground the Church's teaching on religious freedom: "What is more, this doctrine of freedom has roots in divine revelation, and for this reason Christians are bound to respect it all the more conscientiously" (*DH* 9). But this theological claim does not receive any extensive treatment because its purpose is to place the Church unambiguously on the juridical side of modern democracies and the Establishment Clause. The document is primarily juridical, not theological. Guided by the principle that separates church from state, *DH* abandons the once-held sacral order that established the Roman Catholic Church as the one and true religion.

The juridical strength and its universal secular appeal uncover the central theological weakness in the failure to develop a theology of freedom, especially with respect to how the Church addresses the religious freedom of its members. This omission is not without practical and political consequences. It leaves the institution open to the critique that what the Church preaches and practices *ad extra*, does not correspond to what it preaches and practices *ad intra*. There is a need not only to clarify the Church's teaching on religious freedom *ad intra*, but also to address unreconciled tensions between affirming the right to religious freedom and other human rights. Affirming an integral ecology of human rights paves the way in this direction.

Without rejecting that, for many faith-filled persons, religious freedom is the cornerstone of other rights, a better ecology of rights and cooperation among human rights activists must be birthed. This ecology would seek integration rather than separation among proponents of traditionally conceived inalienable rights such as religious freedom and those advocating for other human rights (sometimes characterized as positive rights, meaning rights that require the support of other people or institutions, such as medical care, food, or education). Such an ecology would further unfold the universal appeal of *DH*, overcome current tensions and divisions, and increase mutual respect for the distinct ways that the human rights tradition defends human dignity, especially the dignity of poor, marginalized, and oppressed minorities. As it was in the 1960s, there is great urgency for the Church to affirm freedom from coercion and restraint. In pursuing this venerable path, questions of human conscience formed "under all suitable means" and impacting human lives both *ad extra* and *ad intra* with respect to the Church will need further exploration.

The recent COVID-19 pandemic and the debates on religious freedom surrounding this crisis exemplify the ongoing relevance of *DH*. The question of whether governments could require vaccinations as a matter of public health once again reminds us of unresolved questions related to *DH*'s teaching on religious freedom, governmental responsibilities, and public order. Debates around religious freedom and vaccinations have raised numerous lawsuits that appeal to medical conscience and parental rights; many of these arguments invoke as an ally the fundamental right to religious freedom. The issue of vaccination and religious freedom became so heated that it prompted the Vatican's Congregation for the Doctrine of Faith to issue an official statement endorsing the use of vaccines produced from cell lines drawn from tissue of aborted fetuses.

Faintly echoing *DH*'s teaching that "society has the right to defend itself against possible abuses committed on the pretext of freedom of religion" and the "special duty of government to provide this protection" (*DH* 7), the Congregation underscores: "In any case, from the ethical point of view, *the morality of vaccination depends not only on the duty to protect one's own health, but also on the duty to pursue the common good*." Not only did the Vatican's Congregation for the Doctrine of Faith weigh in on the public debates over vaccines, but Pope Francis himself has intervened in this matter: "Being vaccinated with vaccines authorized by the competent authorities is an act of love. And contributing to ensure the majority of people are vaccinated is an act of love—love for oneself, love for one's family and friends, love for all people" (Pope Francis, "Vaccination Is an Act of Love").

THE FUTURE OF RELIGIOUS FREEDOM

In its groundbreaking affirmation that only people—not ideas—have rights, *DH* not only positioned the Church to become a credible defender of persecuted Christian and other religious minorities around the world, but also opened ongoing dialogue around religious freedom and the dignity of all human persons. However, the declaration left some unresolved questions, especially related to the exercise of religious freedom *ad intra*, the reconciliation of religious freedom and other human rights within an integral ecology of human rights, and the question of when governments may have the right to interfere to promote public health and order. Another document from the Council, *Ad Gentes* (*AG*), the Decree on the Missionary Activity of the Church, considered the opportunities and challenges that lie ahead with respect to affirming religious freedom within increasingly diverse, polarized, and secularized societies. This decree on the nature of the Church offers a signpost for how Christians realize their vocation to become ambassadors of Christ (see 2 Cor 5:20).

To be Church is to be missionary. The missionary nature of the Church stems from its vocation to participate in God's own triune missionary and life-giving activity in the world. In the image of God, the Church reaches out into the world as a sign of grace and salvation. This is the central affirmation that we find in *AG*. From this theological perspective, we can understand the Church as a people brought into being by the Holy Spirit and sent forth to witness freely to the life-giving message of Christ. Aligned with ancient theological arguments that attest to the omnipresence of God, *AG* not only affirms the Church as the bearer of Christ's presence and good news. The Church also receives much goodness from the world and, in the words of this decree, is called to "heal," "uplift," and "perfect" whatever goodness comes from all human beings (*AG* 9). Mirroring the central teaching of *DH*, this decree warns against religious coercion, preventing Christians from strong-arming others in fulfilling the Church's missionary nature.

Ad Gentes maps the teaching on the Church's mission by examining six themes: principles of doctrine, mission work itself, the mission of local churches, the work of Christian missionaries, the planning of missionary activity, and finally, the need for Christians to cooperate in proclaiming, teaching, and witnessing to the gospel in accordance with their distinct gifts within the Church. The main purpose of this decree is to highlight the Church's origins in the mission of Jesus Christ and in his *catholic* invocation to proclaim the gospel to all nations (see Matt 28:19). It is in this sense that the Church derives its missionary nature and universal call (*AG* 1).

A document published in 2019 by the Vatican's International Theological Commission (ITC) and titled "Religious Freedom for the Good of All" takes up the central themes of *DH* in ways that resonate with *AG*. Differing from *DH* with respect to its theological emphasis (as opposed to DH's more juridical approach), it examines religious freedom within the context of the Church's missionary nature as explicated in *AG*, the Church's commitment to respect religious freedom, and the ethical imperative to respect human consciences. It addresses the current context of religious freedom, reinforcing central teachings of *DH* on the dignity of all human persons, the juridical prohibition against coercion, and stressing the contribution that respecting religious freedom makes to peace, social order, and the common good.

The ITC document hints at the challenges that will continue to be part of a world marked by political and religious diversity, cautioning against the dangers of atheistic fundamentalism, soft totalitarianism, and theocratic fanaticism. Atheistic fundamentalism undermines religious freedom. Soft totalitarianism tolerates but often considers religious affiliation and expression as an obstacle to political citizenship. Theocratic fanaticism stems from religious radicalization and weaponizes religion. In what could be interpreted as foresight into the future considering these social and religious contexts that undermine religious freedom, the document invites the praxis of "conviviality of humanity" within states and among religious communities.

In its concluding chapter, the theological commission explicitly turns its attention to mining the implications of the Church's teaching on religious freedom (*DH*) in relation to the Church's self-understanding as missionary (*AG*). It sheds light on some of the ways that the Roman Catholic Church can continue to advocate for religious freedom even while remaining faithful to its evangelical mission. In relating religious freedom and the Church's missionary activity, it discusses four themes: (1) the free witness of the love of God, (2) the Church's proclamation of religious freedom for all, (3) interreligious dialogue as a path to peace, and (4) the courage to discern authentic religiosity and refute all violence in the name of God.

A synthesis of the key ideas in the final chapter of this document and their ongoing implications are worth referencing as Catholics seek to express their faith within diverse political and religious contexts. First, the freedom of the Church is the freedom to proclaim and actualize mercy. In the present and in the future, this freedom can best be guaranteed in a *humanistic* environment that promotes cooperation and conviviality. Second, religious plurality will surely remain a reality for the Church and governments around the world. As the document observes, religious freedom is not the goal of evangelization, but it is a central contributing factor, especially given the religious pluralism and interreligious nature of societies around the world. Seen from a Christian perspective, affirming religious differences in accordance with distinct ways of being human within and outside the Church can be read as the "relational form of evangelical love," and essential to defending the very value of religious freedom. Finally, religious freedom and peace are closely linked. The document fittingly rejects the political manipulation and violent misuse of religion. As we look to the future of religion and the credibility of religious communities to affirm freedom *from* coercion and freedom *to* believe and practice, this document reminds Christians of the need to remain ever vigilant and self-critical against the temptation to weaponize faith and religious practices. Essentially, the Church is called to freely evangelize (not proselytize). But the Church must practice what it preaches in a world where the virtue of prudence and the reconciliation of human rights and differences need to be cultivated.

CONCLUSION

As discussed in this chapter, the Second Vatican Council's Declaration on Religious Freedom (*DH*) represents a significant development and contribution to the subject of religious freedom. The American Jesuit theologian John Courtney Murray persuaded Church leaders to abandon a position of religious privilege enjoyed within a sacral view of society and embrace instead one that acknowledges the separation of church and state and the secular value of democratic principles. In this sense, Murray built the bridge for the Church to cross from the belief that "error has no rights," to "only people—not ideas—have rights." Challenges remain in efforts to expand the meaning of religious freedom and further historize it individually, communally, and socially. The Church must continue to affirm the juridical concept of religious freedom and affirm it as a human and civic right, but it must also unequivocally embrace it as a theological concept *ad intra* and deepen its relevance for the baptized members of its body. In this way, the Church will become a more effective model of this teaching in the world today. Finally, conversations and debates surrounding religious freedom must continue. Further changes likely lie ahead with respect to reconciling religious freedom, other human rights, and the law. But these changes need not be feared. As the historian John W. O'Malley invites us to consider: "Sometimes change is required precisely in order to remain faithful to the tradition. It has in that way been operative in the church from the beginning."

FOR FURTHER READING

Clemmer, Don. "We Don't Understand Religious Freedom. COVID-19 Proved It." *U.S. Catholic*, June 8, 2021. https://uscatholic.org/articles/202106/we-dont-understand-religious-freedom-covid-19-proved-it/. Accessed March 17, 2023.

Díaz, Miguel. "An Unfinished Project: John Courtney Murray, Religious Freedom, and Unresolved Tensions in Contemporary American Society." *Loyola University Law Journal* 50, no.1 (Fall 2018): 1–23. https://loyola-chicago-law-journal.scholasticahq.com/article/77131-an-unfinished-project-john-courtney-murray-religious-freedom-and-unresolved-tensions-in-contemporary-american-society. Accessed February 20, 2024.

Francis, Pope. "Vaccination Is an Act of Love." Cited in Devin Watkins. "Pope Francis Urges People to Get Vaccinated against COVID-19." *Vatican News*, August 18, 2021. https://www.vaticannews.va/en/pope/news/2021-08/pope-francis-appeal-covid-19-vaccines-act-of-love.html. Accessed March 17, 2023.

Griffin, Leslie. "*Dignitatis Humanae*." In *Modern Catholic Social Teaching: Commentaries & Interpretations*, edited by Kenneth R. Himes, 244–65. Washington, DC: Georgetown University Press, 2005.

International Theological Commission. "Religious Freedom for the Good of All: Theological Approaches and Contemporary Challenges." March 21, 2019. https://www.vatican.va/roman_curia/congregations/cfaith/cti_documents/rc_cti_20190426_liberta-religiosa_en.html#The_perspective_of_Dignitatis_Humanae_in_its_Time_and_Today. Accessed March 17, 2023.

Madera, Adelaide, ed. "The Crisis of Religious Freedom in the Age of COVID-19 Pandemic." *Laws*, special issue (October 2021). https://www.mdpi.com/books/book/4495. Accessed February 20, 2024.

Murray, John Courtney, SJ. "The Declaration on Religious Freedom." In *War, Poverty, Freedom: The Christian Response*, 3–16. Vol. 15 of *Concilium*, edited by Franz Böckle. New York: Paulist Press, 1966.

———. "Religious Freedom." In *The Documents of Vatican II*, edited by Walter M. Abbott, 672–75. New York: Guild, 1966.

Pavan, Pietro. "The Right to Religious Freedom in the Conciliar Declaration." In *Religious Freedom*, edited by Neophytos Edelby and Teodoro Jiménez-Urresti, 37–52. New York: Paulist Press, 1966.

7

LAITY AND CHRISTIAN EDUCATION

Hosffman Ospino

Many lay Catholics who lived prior to the Second Vatican Council (1962–65) jokingly summarized their relationship to the institutional Church in three words: pay, pray, and obey. The quick formula may draw a few smiles, yet the irony of the humor should not go unnoticed. It points to the reality that in many ecclesial quarters little was expected of laypeople in terms of expressing their voices on matters related to the faith and how the Church should do its work, or any active participation in the Church's evangelizing mission beyond what they could do in their immediate spaces (e.g., homes and parishes). Much less was expected in terms of assuming responsibilities inside and outside ecclesiastical structures in the name of the Church. All these were presumed to be primarily functions of the ordained and the consecrated. The laity supported and helped when invited—and if necessary.

For four centuries, the Catholic Church had been engaged in the implementation of reforms introduced by the Council of Trent (1545–63) in response to the rise of Protestant Christianity. During those four centuries, much attention was given to affirming the centrality and powers of the papacy, a conversation that crystallized at the First Vatican Council (1869–70). As Catholics argued about the importance of the seven sacraments, some of which were challenged by Protestant theologians, the liturgy and the role of priests dominated many Catholic conversations. Concerns about poor preaching, lack of discipline among priests, and ignorance of the faith among the faithful led to centuries of emphasizing a stronger formation of the clergy so they could celebrate, preach, and lead well. During the centuries prior to Vatican II, much of Catholic energy was focused on intra-ecclesial affairs, the role of the ordained, and a rather staunch defense of doctrines and structures. Even the large missionary movements that emerged after the Council of Trent, and the planting of Catholic communities in lands beyond Europe, were driven by a fervent desire to make the institution stronger.

What about attending to the laity? One could technically argue that everything that church structures and leaders do is at the service of accompanying the baptized on their spiritual journeys while they grow in their relationship with Jesus Christ. From that perspective, the laity is always at the heart of the Church's self-understanding and mission. However, a more stimulating question is: How does the Church understand the nature and role of the laity? Vatican II had much to say about this. Church historian Mark S. Massa asserts that "the council fathers began their theological consideration of 'Church' not with a discussion of the structures and government of the central hierarchy centered on the pope, but with the notion of the Church as a 'people on pilgrimage.'" All of us are part of that pilgrimage and all play an important role.

If the laity are perceived mainly as passive recipients of pastoral services, or just as helpers of the ordained and the consecrated as they evangelize, then expectations about their potential, roles, and contributions are likely to be minimal. Calls to educate laypeople through catechesis and theological formation for agency and participation, inside and outside church structures, may be received with suspicion. Seeing laypeople doing activities that were traditionally done by ordained and vowed religious pastoral agents can be interpreted as intrusive, even threatening. Mindful that most leadership roles in the Church have historically been held by men, the presence of women in some of those roles, or the sheer discussion about the possibility of women exercising liturgical and governance roles traditionally reserved to ordained men, can be a source of tension.

If all laypeople, without exception, are understood as equal members of the people of God empowered by God's Holy Spirit through baptism, called to participate in Jesus Christ's threefold ministry of prophecy, priesthood, and governance, and are welcome to share their many gifts with the institutional Church and the rest of the world to build God's reign, then...

REPOSITIONING THE LAITY

Among the various shifts that Vatican II introduced while providing a roadmap for the Catholic Church in our day, centering baptism and thus repositioning the laity vis-à-vis the Church's evangelizing mission were perhaps among the most exciting ones.

The Dogmatic Constitution on the Church, *Lumen Gentium*, made it clear that the lay faithful "are by baptism made one body with Christ and are constituted among the People of

God; they are in their own way made sharers in the priestly, prophetical, and kingly functions of Christ; and they carry out for their own part the mission of the whole Christian people in the Church and in the world" (§31). In privileging the image of people of God, born in the waters of baptism, sustained by God's word, nurtured by sacramental grace, and guided by the same Holy Spirit, the Council reminded us about the common ground where all apostolic activity in the Church begins. Although there are different vocations among the baptized and there are different responsibilities in the process of carrying out the Church's evangelizing mission, everything starts with our baptismal identity and the call to holiness.

The Council masterfully repositions the laity by retrieving a rich theology of baptism that has been central to the Christian tradition and by making some important corrections in terms of how we understand the role of the laity in history. Laywomen and -men are not simply passive recipients of pastoral services, or bystanders in the work of evangelization, or mere helpers of the ordained and the consecrated when a need arises. The laity are neither above nor below the ordained in terms of their dignity as disciples. From the perspective of the Church as people of God, there is no such thing as being "in the Church" and "outside the Church." The Council offers a vision of the laity as active and responsible agents of the Church's mission as an expression of their baptismal identity, working shoulder to shoulder with the ordained and those called to consecrated life, striving to be holy in their everyday existence, and equally accountable for the transformation of the world.

Vatican II's Decree on the Apostolate of the Laity, *Apostolicam Actuositatem*, expands on all these convictions. The decree speaks of the laity's apostolic action as "right and duty" (§3). The lay apostolate is neither accidental nor derivative. It is grounded in the union of the laity with Christ through baptism and sustained by the constant work of the Holy Spirit who confers on the faithful "special gifts" (§3).

Apostolicam Actuositatem insists repeatedly that the lay faithful "exercise their apostolate both in the Church and in the world, in both the spiritual and the temporal orders" (§5). This is an important affirmation because it reiterates the traditional conviction that laywomen and -men are called to witness their baptismal identity in the many realms in which their lives unfold, yet it does it while lifting up the ecclesial dimensions of their apostolic activity, including the exercise of ministry within ecclesiastical structures.

Allow me a short detour. *Apostolicam Actuositatem*, and the rest of the Vatican II documents, continue to use dualistic language such as "the church/the world," "spiritual realm/temporal order" or "sacred/secular." Such language reflects an old cosmology, common in the Bible and in some traditional theologies, that tends to understand the world as divided into realms, often in some form of conflict. The language becomes problematic when categories such as "the spiritual," "the sacred" and "the holy" are treated as synonymous with the institutional Church or the work of people who are ordained or consecrated, thus assuming that those who are not living their baptismal identity inside ecclesial structures may not be sufficiently spiritual, sacred, or holy. Likewise, many assume that, because the laity are not ordained and the vast majority are not vowed religious, they have little to say or do within the ecclesial structures, which may have been a widespread conviction prior to the Council. While the Church of Jesus Christ transcends human and historical expressions, the Church as an institution is in the world and the baptized *are* the world insofar as no one can live outside history. Too much emphasis on differentiating church from world, sacred from secular may prevent us from fully appreciating the vocation of the laity.

Apostolicam Actuositatem charges the laity with the responsibility of sanctifying the world: "All those things which make up the temporal order, namely, the good things of life and the prosperity of the family, culture, economic matters, the arts and professions, the laws of the political community, international relations, and other matters of this kind, as well as their development and progress, not only aid in the attainment of man's ultimate goal but also possess their own intrinsic value" (§7).

This is an important development in the theology of the laity that we receive from the Council. All the baptized receive the necessary gifts from the Holy Spirit to give witness as disciples of Jesus Christ and to transform the realities in which we live. Yes, the world is sanctified through sacramental grace and the ministry of the word, both closely associated with the vocation of the baptized who are ordained. But these are not the only ways in which the world is sanctified. Laypeople sanctify the world by striving for holiness, forming strong families, working for the common good (see §§8–9), denouncing error and evil (see §§6–7), serving others with charity (see §8), among others. The witness of the homemaker is as important and necessary as that of the bishop; the effort of the baptized parent teaching the faith to children at home or that of the baptized nurse caring for the sick person in whom she sees the face of Christ is as meaningful, central, and sanctifying as that of the missionary who goes to a faraway land to announce the good news of the gospel.

While it is expected that individual baptized persons are to engage in apostolic work to advance the Church's evangelizing mission—and most do this through witness in their specific contexts—*Apostolicam Actuositatem* acknowledges the value and potential of apostolic work done by lay associations (see §15), which is crucial to evangelization and is to be integrated into the Church's larger evangelizing efforts (see §23).

The decree recognizes the importance of apostolic groups "because the apostolate must often be performed by way of common activity both the Church communities and the various spheres" (§18). The Council affirms the centuries-old tradition of laypeople associating to engage in apostolic activity. These groups do not necessarily need to do or look the same: "Some set before themselves the broad apostolic purpose of the Church; others aim to evangelize and sanctify in a special way. Some purpose to infuse a Christian spirit into the temporal order; others bear witness to Christ in a special way through works of mercy and charity" (§19). In the past, many similar lay groups evolved into formal religious orders as they embraced consecrated life. Here, however, we see a clear affirmation of the vocation to the lay apostolate. Laypeople are to live and practice the gospel as laypeople without needing to be consecrated or ordained. The Council recognizes how the Holy Spirit is leading the Church into a new era of lay apostolic and ministerial activity, which in turn has enriched our Catholic understanding of the ordained priesthood and religious life, yielding many fruits over the last sixty years.

In this context, the education of the laity has emerged as a top priority for the Catholic Church. The Council asserted: "The apostolate can attain its maximum effectiveness only through a diversified and thorough formation" (*Apostolicum Actuositatem* 28). Furthermore, the Council's Declaration on Christian Education, *Gravissimum Educationis*, strongly affirmed a double right. On the one hand, every person "of every race, condition and age, since they enjoy the dignity of a human being, have an inalienable right to an education" (§1). On the other hand, all Christians "have a right to a Christian education" (§2). From this perspective, the Council understands that without education not only human progress and well-being will be hindered, but also the Church's evangelizing mission in the world—a responsibility of every baptized person—can be undermined (cf. *Gravissimum Educationis* §12). Furthermore, Catholic schools, colleges, and universities and faculties of sacred sciences are at the service of the baptized—the vast majority of them laywomen and -men—preparing them to transform the world and to grow as disciples of Jesus Christ (§§8–12).

Let's place this observation in a larger context. By the year 1900, about 21 percent of adults in the world were literate (i.e., they knew how to read and write); in 1960 the rate increased to 42 percent. In 2023, it is approximately 86 percent. More progress was made in this area in one century than in an entire millennia. Educated Catholics are more likely to pursue formal education and ask questions, engage in critical conversations, seek participation, and ultimately expect treatment from their leaders that honors their experience, agency, and contributions. We can say something similar about Catholics who are well-formed in their faith. Any contemporary understanding of the laity and their role in the Church must reflect the realities of people living in the twenty-first century rather than those of people living in the nineteenth century or earlier.

HARVESTING THE FIRSTFRUITS

Since the Second Vatican Council, Catholics have witnessed a whirlwind of developments in terms of how we understand the nature, place, and role of the laity in the Church's evangelizing mission, and how laywomen and -men have stepped forward to own their baptismal identity and ecclesial vocation. Those developments need to be considered alongside the dramatic changes in our world during recent decades and the fast pace with which many of them have occurred. We are regularly confronting new ways of understanding who we are as individuals, families, communities, societies, and nations; the role of religion in society continues to shift; the rise of technology, new forms of communication, and the influence of social media have redefined relationships; scientific developments and our understanding of the universe leave us speechless every day; new pedagogies, new educational platforms, and how people understand the purposes of education have thrust us into a world of experimentation for which our ecclesial structures were not necessarily prepared. Sometimes, it feels that our Catholic catechetical programs, schools, seminaries, and some universities were created for a world that does not exist any longer. Keep in mind that it has been only sixty years since the Council!

To put things in perspective, four hundred years lapsed between the Council of Trent and Vatican II, which is a rather generous period to implement a council. Despite the many reforms that emerged from Trent, a good number of them focusing on doctrine and a reassessment of practices related to ordained ministry, the ecclesial and theological understanding of clerical life changed rather little. If a priest from the sixteenth century traveled in time into the early twentieth century, except for some canonical and cultural adaptations, he would have been able to exercise his ministry without much disruption. This is not necessarily the case for the laity since Vatican II.

Let me highlight five developments that are breathtaking, yet fascinating. These observations apply primarily to the context of Catholicism in the United States of America.

Firstly, laywomen and -men studying theology, ministry, and religion sciences. Today we take for granted that most students in universities and pastoral institutes in the United States are laypeople. Although that is not the case in many parts of the world, especially where Catholicism is growing more rapidly today as in the case of Africa and Latin America, most likely these regions will experience a similar phenomenon. Several seminaries dedicated to the formation of future priests have established programs for lay theological and ministerial formation. Several university-based programs of ministerial formation form candidates for the priesthood alongside laywomen and -men. This was practically unthinkable a hundred years ago! Although a handful of laymen were welcomed into theology programs, women were not. The Sister Formation Movement in the United States challenged the status quo by creating programs of theological formation for vowed religious women. Soon, laywomen were welcomed into these programs. Hundreds of theological and ministerial programs are sponsored by dioceses, parishes, and organizations throughout the country. Catholicism in the United States benefits significantly from having one of the most educated adult populations and one of the largest contingents of theologically trained laywomen and -men in the world.

Secondly, emerging theologies of the laity and by the laity. Most Catholic theologians in the United States today are laywomen and -men writing, teaching, researching, and serving in ministerial positions and other professional settings. This is a dramatic change compared to 1946, when the Catholic Theological Society of America was established only with priests and for priests. Only priests taught theology at the time, mostly in the context of seminaries. The emergence of a lay majority among Catholic theologians has opened important doors to engage in creative conversations—through the eyes of the laity—about what it means to be a layperson in our particular historical moment. At the same time, lay scholars are doing important work reflecting on the importance of ordained and consecrated life, adding important insights into our ecclesial understanding of these vocations. As lay theologians write and teach largely in university settings (notice the important shift in context), they draw from their own experiential wells addressing topics that perhaps in the past did not have the same centrality in the world of theological reflection as they have today: family life, parenting, balance between life and work, political participation, embodied existence, equality and inclusion, care of the created order, illness, aging, the influence of technology as we raise the next generation, and so on.

Thirdly, the rise of lay ecclesial ministry. The Second Vatican Council recognized that there are laypeople—single and married—who dedicate their lives permanently or temporarily to serve in ecclesial ministry at various levels (see *Apostolicam Actuositatem* §22). Such service is their vocation and an actualization of their baptismal identity. Catholics in the United States speak of lay ecclesial ministers. The U.S. Catholic bishops articulated their understanding of this important ministry in the life of the Church in their 2005 document *Co-workers in the Vineyard of the Lord: A Resource for Guiding the Development of Lay Ecclesial Ministry*. Tens of thousands of laywomen and -men throughout the country sustain the Church's evangelizing mission as pastoral associates, directors of faith formation, theologians, canon lawyers, chancellors, and parochial administrators with faculties to preach, baptize, and witness weddings, among other forms of service. All of them work alongside priests, deacons, and other pastoral leaders. The 1983 Code of Canon Law, several documents from the Vatican, and most recently Pope Francis with his *motu proprio, Spiritus Domini* (2021) opening the ministries of Lector and Acolyte to women, and his *motu proprio, Antiquum Ministerium* (2021) establishing the ministry of catechist, have paved the way for a stronger and more significant presence of the laity in ecclesial structures.

Fourthly, the growing influence of new ecclesial movements. It is practically impossible to speak of Catholic evangelization in our day without acknowledging the impact and potential of the new ecclesial movements. Movements such as the Catholic Charismatic Renewal, the Neocatechumenal Way, Cursillo, Focolare, and Worldwide Marriage Encounter, among many others, sustain the spiritual life and apostolic vocation of millions of Catholics throughout the world. These are movements within the Church primarily constituted and driven by lay Catholics, although with an important presence of ordained and consecrated people. These movements rise as a true manifestation of the work of the Holy Spirit today. They are free and rather flexible associations of Catholics that often follow baptized leaders whose charisms are perceived as sources of inspiration for Christian discipleship. The ecclesial movements are an invitation to live the gospel with a sense of radical commitment in *lo cotidiano* (everyday life) without having to abandon one's lay status. In many parts of the world, the new ecclesial movements are the major source of spiritual and pastoral accompaniment for Catholics. They do missionary work, provide sound catechesis, advance major initiatives of adult faith formation, foster vocations to ecclesial ministry, and sustain Catholic identity. In some parts of the world, they have become the most viable alternative after parish life has collapsed. In the United States, they often work in close collaboration with Catholic parishes and Catholic educational institutions (e.g., campus ministry). Alongside the new ecclesial movements, laypeople continue to associate in confraternities, fraternal orders, third orders, apostolates, Catholic associations, secular institutes, and other forms of communal life. There is no doubt that Vatican II inspired a new era of lay ecclesial involvement that is yielding many fruits.

Fifthly, the rise of the digital world and new technologies, and defining roles for the laity. Vatican II addressed the question of social communications through the media in its decree *Inter Mirifica*. One of the major concerns raised by the decree was the growing influence of the media shaping people's opinion on moral values, the idea of the common good, and the understanding of what it means to be human. *Inter Mirifica* called for the exercise of responsibility in the use of media (§11), always seeking what is true and good (§7), and remaining aware that the media can be instrumentalized to promote evil (§§2, 7, 9, 11). The decree called for ecclesiastical leaders and laypeople to be diligent in promoting the good press (§14) and maintain a vigilant eye on any misuse of the media (§19). When referring to the media, those at the Council in the 1960s mainly had "the press, movies, radio, television and the like" (§1) in mind. Just a few decades later, the world would enter a major historical revolution triggered by mass access to the internet, the invention of cellular technology, the omnipresence of social media, and the rise of artificial intelligence, among other developments. The concerns raised by *Inter Mirifica* seem to pale before the new concerns these technologies are placing before us today; the recommendations the decree proposed barely meet the new complex realities that are emerging. It is in this brave new world where the laity are leading the way, especially young lay Catholics who are digital natives. Perhaps no other historical moment has made more urgent the need for the institutional Church to listen to young people than today. We seem to have entered a moment in which not seriously listening to the laity on this and other questions and working alongside young laywomen and -men may render the institutional Church obsolete and irrelevant in a fast-changing world.

CONCLUSION

There is much to affirm and celebrate about lay Catholics living their Christian discipleship in more intentional ways during the last sixty years. We live in a new era of Catholic ecclesial life in which laywomen and -men have moved from ancillary and more peripheric roles to forms of evangelical and ministerial protagonism—inside and outside ecclesial structures—that are injecting the Church with new life. Yet, the reflection continues. Among some areas of growth in that reflection, I propose the following five: (1) integration of the new lay ecclesial movements in the regular ministry of the Church; (2) further support of formation of lay ecclesial ministers and catechists; (3) widespread recognition of the vocation to lay ecclesial ministry and more permanent forms of ministerial authorization as well as liturgical commissioning; (4) spaces and opportunities for laywomen and -men to preach within the liturgical life of the Church; (5) more structured participation in synodal conversations, theological consultations, and ecclesial governance.

FOR FURTHER READING

Cahoy, William John, ed. *In the Name of the Church: Vocation and Authorization of Lay Ecclesial Ministry*. Collegeville, MN: Liturgical Press, 2012.

Cattaro, Gerald Michael, and Charles J. Russo, eds. *Gravissimum Educationis: Golden Opportunities in American Catholic Education 50 Years after Vatican II*. Lanham, MD: Rowman & Littlefield, 2015.

Hahnenberg, Edward P. *Ministries: A Relational Approach*. New York: Crossroad, 2003.

Leckey, Dolores R. *The Laity and Christian Education: Apostolicam Actuositatem, Gravissimum Educationis*. Mahwah, NJ: Paulist Press, 2006.

Massa, Mark S. *The American Catholic Revolution: How the Sixties Changed the Church Forever*. New York: Oxford University Press, 2010.

O'Malley, John W. *What Happened at Vatican II.* Cambridge, MA: Belknap Press of Harvard University Press, 2010.

Ospino, Hosffman. *Called to Witness Hope: The Ministry of Catechist.* Mahwah, NJ: Paulist Press, 2023.

Wood, Susan K., and Michael Downey, eds. *Ordering the Baptismal Priesthood: Theologies of Lay and Ordained Ministry.* Collegeville, MN: Liturgical Press, 2003.

Conclusion

A NEW PENTECOST

Synodality as a Springtime of Vatican II

Sr. Nathalie Becquart, xmcj

As he convoked Vatican II, Pope John XXIII prayed that the Council would become like "a new Pentecost." This powerful phrase connects the life of the Church to its birth: the outpouring of the Holy Spirit upon the apostles that sent them out on mission. At the same time, Pentecost is not merely a historical event that happened two millennia ago. It is a springtime that must be constantly renewed, so that the Church's mission can bear fruit in each time and place on the Church's pilgrimage through history toward God's kingdom.

The Council emphasized this journey of God's people as the inner dynamism of a church that goes forward to walk with the whole of humanity on the path toward the kingdom of God. In our day, Pope Francis has called us to renew the way that the Church walks together—both the way we walk with each other within the Church, as well as our way of walking with everyone outside of the Church. Synodality is this path of "walking together" that happens on both levels. It is both *ad intra* and *ad extra*, such that there is no longer a separation between the inner life of the Church and its missionary fruitfulness. Synodality links the core dynamism of the Church with its constant call to go out of itself: "The pilgrim Church is missionary by her very nature," as *Ad Gentes* 2 highlights.

Pope Francis has called us to be a more *synodal Church*. In October 2015, on the 50th anniversary of the creation of the Synod of Bishops, he made the bold and prophetic statement that: "It is precisely this path of synodality which God expects of the Church of the third millennium." This means that synodality is not just the key to the Church in the twenty-first century, but for the next thousand years! In a way synodality is the vocation of the Church for this millennium. In this sense, synodality is a paradigm shift from an image of the Church as a vertical pyramid, focused primarily on the top-down authority of the hierarchy, to the Church as a communion of brothers and sisters in Christ together on mission as baptized people called to be missionary disciples.

Synodality is a dynamic vision of the identity of the Church in history, in which the charisms given by the Holy Spirit can shine in each person without exception. Vatican II was a watershed moment that laid the groundwork for this transformative renewal of our way of being church. The Council insisted on the active participation of all the baptized, the apostolate of the laity, and an ecclesiology of communion uniting all members of the Body of Christ. Today, we are experiencing a new springtime of the Council, entering a fresh phase of receiving its key teachings all these decades later.

The word *synodality* does not appear in any of the sixteen documents of the Council's teachings. Yet in those documents, the Council frequently refers to itself as a "Synod," since the word *council* in Latin translates as *synod* in Greek. For example, the opening paragraph of *Lumen Gentium* speaks of Vatican II as "this Sacred Synod gathered together in the Holy Spirit." Even though the word *synodality* is not used by the Council, the documents of Vatican II provide a blueprint for the synodal renewal of the Church. The Australian theologian Ormond Rush underlines in an insightful formula that "synodality is the Second Vatican Council in a nutshell." The concept of "synodality" synthesizes many key elements of the Council's vision, namely participation, dialogue, the signs of the times, and the *sensus fidei* of the whole people of God. In this same vein, Italian theologian Piero Coda has called the synodal process from 2021 to 2024 the "most important event" in the life of the Church since Vatican II, since for the first time in the 2000-year history of the Church, the entire people of God has been given the opportunity to take part.

Through the experience of the synodal process that the Church has embarked upon from 2021 to 2024, we have come to better understand the teachings of the Council in the context of today's world. The path of synodality is an opportunity to receive more deeply the Council's teachings and to put them into practice at this stage of history. Even if we are now several decades after the conclusion of Vatican II in 1965, there is still much to be implemented of the Council's vision. The renewal brought about by the Council sought to be at the same time an *aggiornamento* and a *ressourcement*, meaning an updating that happens by going back to the sources of the Church's life and mission. The current synodal updating of the Church today takes place in the framework of the Council's project of *aggiornamento* begun sixty years ago. If the birth of the Church took place by the descent of the Holy Spirit at Pentecost, we are becoming increasingly aware that the Holy Spirit has not ceased to be at work in the life of the Church and the world in every stage of history, including today. The experience of synodality is making us more and more conscious that the Holy

Spirit can speak not only through the pastors of the Church, but also through all the members of the baptized and even all people of good will, especially those belonging to groups that are often marginalized in some way, such as women, young people, and people in poverty.

This calls for a "listening Church" in which everyone is called to listen and learn. It is in this same sense Pope Francis, in that 2015 address marking a half century of the synod of bishops, stated,

> A synodal Church is a Church which listens, which realizes that listening "is more than simply hearing." It is a mutual listening in which everyone has something to learn. The faithful people, the college of bishops, the Bishop of Rome: all listening to each other, and all listening to the Holy Spirit, the "Spirit of truth" (Jn 14:17), in order to know what he "says to the Churches" (Rev 2:7).

This listening style is the call for the Church to listen to the peripheries, to the voices of those who are suffering, and even to the cry of the earth. A synodal Church is a church of local churches, a Church "out of every tribe, tongue, people and nation," as described by the title of Chapter 5 of the *Synthesis Report* of the first session of the assembly of the Synod of Bishops in October 2023. This entails a process of globalization and de-Europeanization of the Church's thinking and working, so that the rich cultural diversity of all God's people can be put at the service of the common mission entrusted to all of us. In a polarized world that is marked by conflicts around the globe, the Church plays a vital role as a sign and instrument of unity in diversity. The vocation of the Church is to be "a sign and instrument both of a very closely knit union with God and of the unity of the whole human race," as *Lumen Gentium* 2 puts it. Doing our mission today also means finding ways of engaging with the digital continent, in an era of rapid change that Pope Francis has characterized as a change of era.

As part of the synodal process of the entire Church, I have been privileged to participate in Continental Assemblies that have taken place in Oceania, Asia, the Middle East, Africa, and also in the first session of the Synod of Bishops in October 2023 in Rome. I have personally witnessed how we contemplated the work of the Holy Spirit in these gatherings. In a spirit of prayer, using the method of conversation in the Spirit, the fruits of synodality can be powerfully experienced. We can already see how the Church's journey on the path of synodality is bearing fruit at the grassroots level, fostering communion and participation of the whole people of God for the mission of the Church in the world today. With this synod, we experience a new phase of the reception of the Second Vatican Council opened by Pope Francis's pontificate. Moreover, this synod as an experience of the Spirit is not only rooted in the Second Vatican Council but also expresses a way to unfold the outcomes of the Council and understand better the documents of the Council that are reshaping the Church so it may embody at all levels those three key words highlighted by the synod: communion, participation, mission.

Throughout his pontificate, Pope Francis has focused on *mission*: how to be a more missionary church to better serve the people of the earth in the context of the world today. This is why we are striving to live out this call to synodality. It is because at this stage in the reception of Vatican II, as we have seen through the various Synods of Bishops that have taken place since, the Church has discerned that synodality is the way of being a missionary church today. This does not involve cutting the Church off from her roots, but rather living out more intentionally her deepest identity by responding to the call of God amid the world today. The Church is in constant need of conversion and renewal to be faithful to its most profound calling, so that its mission can bear fruit in each new generation.

Vatican II was a *kairos* moment in the life of the Church, in which the Holy Spirit planted seeds to bear fruit for the life of the world. All popes since the Council have highlighted how the Second Vatican Council is a roadmap for the Church. Let us keep in mind especially this statement from Pope Benedict XVI in a catechesis he offered during his general audience on October 10, 2012: "The documents of Vatican Council II are, even in our own time, a compass guiding the ship of the Church as she sails on the open seas, amidst tempests or peaceful waves, to reach her destination."

This book is a true gift to introduce new generations to the Second Vatican Council. May the readers have a way not only to read about the Council but also to taste its flavor. As with the synodal process, there is also an opportunity for each baptized to experience something of "the Council's style" or Council's spirit. Today, the Church is called to walk with the entire family of humanity to work together for the good of our common home on the path to God's kingdom. The journey of synodality is an experience of being a missionary church of brothers and sisters on a pilgrimage that is open to all. To the extent that we let the Holy Spirit be the protagonist of the synodal renewal of the Church in today's world, we will experience together a new Pentecost in our lives today.

FOR FURTHER READING

Coda, Piero, in Fabio Colagrande. "Sinodo, il teologo Coda: è l'avvenimento più importante dopo il Concilio." *Vatican News*. October 12, 2021.

Rush, Ormond, "Sinodalità, tradizione e consenso." In *Sinodalità e riforma. Una sfida ecclesiale*, ed. Rafael Luciani, Serena Nocetti, and Carlos Schickendantz. Brescia: Queriniana, 2022.

———. *The Vision of Vatican II: Its Fundamental Principles*. Collegeville, MN: Liturgical Press, 2019.

LIST OF CONTRIBUTORS

Sr. Nathalie Becquart, xmcj, is Undersecretary of the General Secretariat of the Synod at the Vatican and member of the Dicastery for Communication. She graduated from HEC School of Management, Paris, studied philosophy and theology at Facultés Loyola Paris (Centre Sèvres), then specialized in ecclesiology at Boston College School of Theology and Ministry. She is the author of numerous publications on synodality and synods, young people and youth ministry, vocations and religious life, the Church and mission.

Christopher M. Bellitto is a professor of history at Kean University in New Jersey. His books include the companion volumes *Renewing Christianity* and *The General Councils* along with *101 Questions and Answers on Popes and the Papacy*. His latest book is *Humility: The Secret History of a Lost Virtue*. He also serves as editor in chief of Brill's Companions to the Christian Tradition and academic editor at large for Paulist Press.

Shaun Blanchard is a lecturer in theology at the University of Notre Dame Australia in Fremantle, Western Australia. He is the author of *The Synod of Pistoia and Vatican II* (Oxford

University Press, 2020). With Ulrich Lehner, Blanchard coedited *The Catholic Enlightenment: A Global Anthology* (Catholic University of America Press, 2021) and, with Richard T. Yoder, coedited *Jansenism: An International Anthology* (Catholic University of America Press, 2024). With Stephen Bullivant, Blanchard cowrote *Vatican II: A Very Short Introduction* (Oxford University Press, 2023).

Kristin Colberg is an associate professor of theology at the College of Saint Benedict and Saint John's University and School of Theology. Her research interests include questions related to Vatican I, Vatican II, ecumenism, and ecclesiology. She serves as a consultant on the theological commission for the synod on synodality and as a member of the Anglican-Roman Catholic Commission (ARCIC). Kristin lives in St. Joseph, Minnesota, with her husband, Shawn, and two daughters, Mary and Catherine.

Miguel H. Díaz is the John Courtney Murray, SJ, University Chair in Public Service at Loyola University Chicago. Dr. Díaz served under President Barack Obama as the ninth U.S. Ambassador to the Holy See. He is a coeditor of the series Disruptive Cartographers: Doing Theology Latinamente. He is the editor of the multiauthored volume 1, *The Word Became Culture*, and the author of volume 3, *Queer God de Amor*. As a public theologian, Professor Díaz regularly engages in print, radio, and television media. He is a contributor to the "Theology en la Plaza" column for the *National Catholic Reporter*. As part of his ongoing commitment to advance human rights globally, he participates in several diplomatic initiatives in Washington, DC, including as a member of the Atlantic Council, a member of the Ambassadors Circle at the National Democratic Institute (NDI), and a member of the Board and Senior Fellow for

Religion and Peacebuilding for the Alliance for Peacebuilding (AfP).

William T. Ditewig is a deacon of the Archdiocese of Washington, DC, ordained in 1990. He has served in a variety of ministries, including five years as the executive director of the Secretariat for the Diaconate at the United States Conference of Catholic Bishops in Washington, DC. He has degrees in philosophy, education, pastoral theology, and a doctorate in theology and religious studies from the Catholic University of America. He teaches and writes extensively on ministry in the Church, especially on Vatican II and the renewed diaconate. His most recent book is *Courageous Humility: Reflections on the Church, Diakonia, and Deacons* (Paulist Press, 2022). A retired navy commander, he and his wife, Diann, have been married for more than fifty years, with four children and fourteen grandchildren.

Rita Ferrone is an award-winning writer and frequent speaker on issues of liturgy and church renewal in the Roman Catholic tradition. She has written for numerous scholarly and popular publications and is a contributing writer and columnist for *Commonweal* magazine. Her articles and essays have been translated into eight languages. Author of several books about liturgy, including *Liturgy: Sacrosanctum Concilium* in the Paulist series Rediscovering Vatican II, she is also a contributor to the international series Vatican II: Legacy and Mandate. Her most recent work is a *Pastoral Guide to Pope Francis's Desiderio Desideravi*.

Hosffman Ospino is professor of theology and religious education at Boston College, School of Theology and Ministry where he is also chair of the Department of Religious Education and Pastoral Ministry. Hosffman has served as the principal investigator for several national studies on Hispanic Catholics. His research explores how faith and culture regularly enter into dialogue in the world of Catholic education as well as in the process of building faith communities in multicultural contexts. He is the author/editor of twenty books and more than 250 articles, academic and general. Among his most recent books are *Called to Witness Hope: The Ministry of Catechist* (Paulist Press, 2023), also available in Spanish, and *Formative Theological Education* (Paulist Press, 2023), coedited with Colleen Griffith. Hosffman is a past president of the Academy of Catholic Hispanic Theologians of the United States (ACHTUS) and currently serves as an officer of the Catholic Theological Society of America (CTSA). He serves on the boards of several national organizations, academic and ministerial, and is actively involved in ministerial activities in the Archdiocese of Boston.

Fr. Ronald D. Witherup, PSS, is a former superior general of the Society of the Priests of Saint Sulpice (2008–22), a society of diocesan priests dedicated to priestly formation. A recent past president of the Catholic Biblical Association of America, he holds a doctorate in biblical studies from Union Theological Seminary in Richmond, Virginia, as well as degrees in spirituality and theology. He recently served as a visiting professor at the Pontifical Biblical Institute in Rome. Father Witherup has authored or edited some twenty-five books, including two studies of *Dei Verbum*, the Dogmatic Constitution on Divine Revelation, and most recently from Paulist Press, *Galatians: Life in the New Creation* (2020), *Scripture and Tradition in the Letters of Paul* (2021), and an updated edition of Raymond E. Brown's *The Critical Meaning of the Bible* (2023), to commemorate the twenty-fifth anniversary of Brown's death.

Stephanie M. Wong is an assistant professor in the Department of Theology and Religious Studies at Villanova University. As a comparative theologian, she teaches Christian theology as well as East Asian religions (especially Confucianism and Buddhism). Her research attends to the development of Chinese Catholic theology and interreligious relations in China. She has published in journals and volumes on Chinese Christianity, World Christianity, and interreligious studies. She serves in a range of academic societies in leadership of academic units on Chinese Christianity and Comparative Theology at the American Academy of Religion and Catholic Theological Society of America. Beyond academia, she serves as a board member for Interfaith Philadelphia and participates in the endeavors of the Holy See's Dicastery of Interreligious Dialogue.